LEARN TO MOVE, MOVE TO LEARN!

SENSORIMOTOR EARLY CHILDHOOD ACTIVITY THEMES

Jenny Clark Brack

Foreword by Linda Baker-Nobles

APC

Autism Asperger Publishing Co.
P.O. Box 23173
Shawnee Mission, KS 66283-0173
www.asperger.net

P.O. Box 23173
Shawnee Mission, KS 66283-0173
www.asperger.net

Publisher's Cataloging-in-Publication
(Provided by Quality Books, Inc.)

Brack, Jenny Clark.
    Learn to move--move to learn : sensorimotor early childhood activity themes / Jenny Clark Brack ; foreword by Linda Baker-Nobles.
        p. cm.
        Includes bibliographical references.
        Library of Congress Control Number: 2004112006
        ISBN 1-931282-63-3

    1. Autistic children--Education (Early childhood) 2. Asperger's syndrome--Patients--Education (Early childhood) 3. Early childhood education--Activity programs. 4. Play therapy.   I. Title.

LC4717.5.B73 2004   371.94
                               QBI33-2108

This book is designed in DingleHopper and Helvetica Neue

Managing Editor: Kirsten McBride
Editorial Support: Ginny Biddulph
Cover and Other Illustrations: Gerard Arantowicz

Printed in the United States of America

DEDICATION

*This book is dedicated to my son, Brian,
who has taught me how to have patience,
compassion and joy in every moment.*

*To my mom, for her words of wisdom and
for helping me feel the magic of music.*

And to my husband, Steve, for his loving support.

ACKNOWLEDGMENTS

Special acknowledgment goes to Linda Baker-Nobles, MS OTR/L, for her guidance and teaching; to Phoebe Grindal and David Grindal for their support; and to colleagues and friends at Three Lakes Educational Cooperative for providing a wonderful environment to create and learn.

– Jenny Clark Brack

TABLE OF CONTENTS

BIBLIOGRAPHY AND SUGGESTED READINGS

FOREWORD

Learn to Move, Move to Learn! is an excellent resource for providing "best practice" occupational therapy services to children in preschool and early childhood settings. Jenny brings years of experience in the development of this program and has used the techniques with many children in different settings during her years of practice. It is a wonderful collection of activities that can be used with all children of differing abilities. Moreover, it is easy to understand and is a collaborative, transdisciplinary program that can be implemented by teachers, other professionals, and parents.

Based on the principles of sensory integration, each session in *Learn to Move, Move to Learn!* addresses motor, language, sensory, cognitive and social/emotional skills. For example, children might be learning their letters while simultaneously working on balance, eye-hand coordination, and turn taking. Each of the 50 themes is accompanied by a lesson plan that provides specific ideas for how to implement a succession of seven activities in a group: warm-up, vestibular, proprioceptive, balance, eye-hand coordination, cool-down and fine motor. All activities are designed to be fun and motivating, while simultaneously providing important sensory input, motor development and learning.

In addition to the lesson plans, the book provides a thorough, yet simple explanation of sensory integration that is easily understood by all adults involved in implementing the group activities. Finally, the book is rounded out by sections on adaptive equipment, special needs of children, collaboration, leadership roles and group management – issues that must be addressed to ensure successful outcomes.

In short, *Learn to Move, Move to Learn!* is one of the few complete programs that I have seen that is simple to use, collaborative, inclusive, transdisciplinary, and fun. This book will be a major handbook for occupational therapists working in school settings.

– Linda Baker-Nobles
Associate Professor of Occupational Therapy
Rockhurst University
Kansas City, Missouri

INTRODUCTION

n 1990 after graduating from the University of Kansas, I landed my first job as a school-based occupational therapist for a rural special education cooperative. With a caseload of 50+ students and 5 schools, I found creative ways to utilize best practice techniques while fulfilling IEP requirements. I worked closely with a speech language pathologist in a self-contained EMH (educable mentally handicapped) classroom. We began weekly sessions of a motor-language group. At the same time, I created a fun, safe, and therapeutic preschool group for the early childhood classrooms following a sensory integration model originated by A. Jean Ayres. This proved very effective in helping children make progress.

In the fall of 1994, I transferred to a different rural special education cooperative. It was at this job that the sensory integration preschool groups evolved once again. With the collaboration of a speech language pathologist, Gloria Bowersox, SLP, and staff of a newly developed early childhood classroom, we took my activity ideas from the sensory integration groups, combined them with ideas from the motor-language lab, and related them to a theme from the early childhood teacher's lesson plans. In addition, consistent with the new requirements of IDEA, we created an atmosphere of collaboration and inclusion, which was highly effective for best practice in school-based occupational therapy. At that time, the preschool group was entitled "Integrated Group."

In the fall of 1999 I worked in an even more rural Kansas location with a fantastic, creative, fun group of early childhood staff. I shared my original ideas about "Integrated Group," and for the next four years we evolved the sensory integration group structure into something I had never imagined. Entitled "Ready S.E.T. Go! Sensorimotor Early Childhood Themes," we developed a more transdisciplinary approach, involving occupational therapy, speech therapy, physical therapy, and early childhood special education staff all working together. All the activities related back to the classroom theme, and I added literature as part of the group activities to incorporate more preparation for kindergarten readiness skills. The result was *Learn to Move, Move to Learn!*

PROGRAM PHILOSOPHY

Learn to Move, Move to Learn! is based on four characteristics.

1. The program uses a sensory integration model as a foundation for activity selection.
2. Each group session is theme- and literature-based. In other words, all activities reflect the theme; in addition, a storybook is read to the children as part of the session.
3. A transdisciplinary approach is used, with team members collaborating and sharing treatment roles while working with all the children.
4. All group activities are performed within an inclusive environment.

Sensory Integration Model

The structure of the program follows Ayres' (1979) model of sensory integration. Each group session consists of seven activities. The activities are sequenced so that the first activities address the child's neurological foundation sensory systems, including vestibular, tactile, and proprioceptive processing. These are followed by higher-level skills of balance and eye-hand coordination. Finally, functional skills complete the sequence with children engaging in a focused fine-motor task that results in an end product. In addition, throughout each activity, language, cognitive, and social skills are facilitated.

It is important to note that true sensory integration therapy is focused on child-directed activities where the child is allowed to seek out specific sensory input, generally with the use of suspended equipment. *Learn to Move, Move to Learn!* is adult-directed, in that an adult facilitates the whole group of children by teaching and demonstrating each planned activity and assisting the children in attaining a "just right" challenge. Thus, although the format of each session is based on the sensory integration developmental sequence, it is better described as sensorimotor activities, defined as "the application of specific sensory stimulation through handling or direct stimulation with the purpose of eliciting a desired motor response" (Bundy, Lane, & Murray, 2002, p. 479).

Theme- and Literature-Based

Emergent literacy skills are critical for young children. Literacy is more than reading. It is the ability to communicate through reading, writing and speaking. Planning activities around thematic units provides children with the opportunity to learn in the context of meaningful activities. In addition, when children learn through multiple sensory modalities, they are better able to remember what they learned and generalize their learning to other settings. Storybooks that reflect the theme of a given session allow children to learn emergent literacy skills through facilitated interaction. Storybooks that have rhyming and repeated phrases or colorful illustrations with simple words are recommended as they allow children to participate more directly in the learning experience.

Transdisciplinary

"Transdisciplinary" is defined as an integrated team that collaborates and often shares treatments. That is, members of various disciplines share roles or functions across disciplinary lines in order to provide the best and most efficient services. Team members may include an early childhood educator, physical therapist, speech language pathologist, occupational therapist, music therapist, and perhaps paraeducators, or even parents. Team members will have more time to collaborate about a child simply because they will have simultaneously scheduled therapy time on a routine basis.

This type of service delivery is consistent with the philosophy of helping the whole child. For example, rather than the physical therapist working with a child's gross-motor skills, a speech language pathologist working with a child's language skills, or an early childhood educator working with a child's cognitive and social skills, all team members help a child with all these skills as the need arises. In addition, this type of service delivery allows the early childhood educator to carry out recommendations made by any of the therapists, so that a child will have repeated opportunities to practice specific skills targeting his or her individual needs.

Inclusive Environments

All group sessions take place in early childhood settings that include children with special needs together with typically developing peer models in a child's natural environment. Examples include public and private schools, Head Start programs, early childhood special education classrooms, community preschools, and daycare facilities. This conforms to federal mandates for serving children with special needs in the least restrictive environment. Typically developing peer models benefit from these sensorimotor activity groups as well.

I am grateful to have the opportunity to share these ideas with anyone working with young children, because I envision a "pay if forward" concept: If I can teach 100 adults working with children, they can help 1,000 children. Over the years, many therapists and teachers have expressed an interest in obtaining copies of my lesson plans for each of the themes, prompting me to write *Learn to Move, Move to Learn! Sensorimotor Early Childhood Activity Themes*. Enjoy!!

– Jenny Clark Brack

CHAPTER 1

OVERViEW OF SENSORY SYSTEMS

earn to Move, Move to Learn! uses sensory integration theory and practice, originated by A. Jean Ayres (1979), as the foundation for the group activities that make up the center of this book. Ayres spent over 30 years combining occupational therapy and neuroscience in researching human behavior. Based on her findings, Ayres states in her book *Sensory Integration and the Child*, "Sensory integration is the organization of sensation for use. Our senses give us information about the physical conditions of our body and the environment around us. Sensations flow into the brain like streams flowing into a lake" (p. 5). In other words, sensory integration allows us to gather information and sort it so that we can interact meaningfully to learn and live successful, fulfilling lives.

The sensory systems begin to form before birth and continue to develop rapidly throughout the early childhood years. Our sensory systems include vestibular (movement), proprioception (muscles and joints), tactile (touch), visual (sight), auditory (hearing), olfactory (smell), and gustatory (taste). The auditory, vestibular, proprioceptive, tactile, and visual systems all develop in utero. The vestibular and proprioceptive systems integrate together to help development of posture, balance, muscle tone, and gravitational security as the child grows and achieves developmental milestones such as crawling, pulling to stand, and walking. The tactile and visual systems integrate to help attain nutritional and emotional development for sucking, eating, mother-infant bonding and tactile comfort. All of these skills assimilate as the child grows, and allow for development of body perception, bilateral coordination, motor planning, attention span, and emotional stability. Eventually, higher-level skills come into play from the integration of the previous skills so that the child develops eye-hand coordination and visual perceptual skills. In short, integration of these systems allows humans to function and perform day-to-day tasks.

Sensory processes take place at an unconscious level, occurring simultaneously in the various sensory systems, which have receptors that pick up information that is sent to the brain. The brain stores, sorts, and compares the incoming information from daily experiences and allows us to use it to move, express feelings, have self-esteem, learn, interact with others, and attend to a task.

SENSORY INTEGRATION PROBLEMS

For many individuals, the sensory input is not integrated as smoothly and effortlessly as outlined above, causing problems of varying levels of severity. Thus, sensory integration difficulties can affect a child's daily routine activities, creating problems with mealtime, bath time, playtime, bedtime, transitions, peer interactions, dressing, and learning.

For example, mealtime is usually considered a time for the family to sit down together and enjoy interacting. The child with a sensory integration disorder may become distressed from the food being too hot or too cold, too spicy or too crunchy. The child may have difficulty staying seated and continuously get up from his seat disrupting the mealtime routine.

Similarly, bath time is usually a fun, playful experience for the child with a typical functioning nervous system. However, for the child with a sensory integration disorder, bath time can become a drawn-out battle between the child and the caregiver. The bath water may be too hot or too cold. The washcloth may feel scratchy and upset the child to tears. And hair washing can be a veritable nightmare as the child becomes upset by having her head tipped backward or if water gets on her face or in her ears.

Even playtime, which is enjoyed by most children and is so important for a child's physical and social/emotional development, can cause problems for children with sensory integration problems. These children may avoid playground equipment due to excessive fear of heights and instead prefer to play in the sandbox by themselves, thus avoiding not only social interactions with peers but also physical activity, which otherwise helps strengthen muscles and develop coordination. Further, these children may choose toys that do not challenge their fine-motor skills, as they may become over-reactive and experience feelings of failure if they are unable to correctly use a given toy.

Bedtime rituals are a typical routine for families. When a child has a sensory integration disorder, bedtime can be very difficult. The child may have atypical fears and have difficulty falling asleep. Furthermore, an unusually high activity level before bedtime may make it difficult for her to stay asleep, causing frequent interruptions in her sleep/wake pattern. Sheets may feel too hot, too cold, or too rough. Or pajamas may feel itchy and keep the child from relaxing in order to fall asleep.

Getting dressed in the morning can take twice as long with a child who has a sensory integration/processing disorder. The texture of the material may feel uncomfortable due to tactile processing problems. Loose-fitting clothing can cause a feeling of annoyance and continuously distract the child throughout his day, making it difficult for him to attend to the task at hand.

The child with sensory integration problems may have a meltdown any time there is a change in the daily routine. He may feel out of control and throw himself on the ground, cry, or become oppositional.

School time can also be very difficult for the child with sensory integration disorder. His nervous system may be on red alert throughout the day, causing him to be distracted by sounds or sights, be irritated by a child brushing up against him, or have an excessive need to "get up and go" out of his chair. As a result, learning often takes a back seat for such a child.

The following checklist offers examples of signs and symptoms of sensory integration/processing dysfunction (see reproducible copy in the Appendix, page 151).

Signs and Symptoms of Sensory Integration/Processing Dysfunction

Tactile
- ☐ Dislikes standing in line
- ☐ Bothered by tags on shirts
- ☐ Dislikes playing with messy things
- ☐ Reacts aversively to textured foods
- ☐ Likes only highly textured foods
- ☐ Does not react to falls, scrapes or bumps
- ☐ Touches everything walks touching the wall
- ☐ Constantly puts things in mouth

Proprioceptive
- ☐ Stamps feet or bangs with hands
- ☐ Writes or holds pencil too hard (or too soft)
- ☐ Plays too roughly
- ☐ Seems unaware of body in space – clumsy
- ☐ Handles toys roughly – lots of banging and breaking
- ☐ Deliberately falls or tumbles a lot
- ☐ Chews hard on things
- ☐ Demonstrates poor motor planning in gross-/fine-motor skills

Vestibular
- ☐ Wiggles around during seated activities
- ☐ Craves spinning or swinging
- ☐ Rocks while seated or standing
- ☐ Likes being upside down
- ☐ Is constantly in motion
- ☐ Is afraid of movement
- ☐ Experiences car sickness
- ☐ Avoids playground equipment
- ☐ Fears having head tilted backward (e.g., hair washing)
- ☐ Is afraid to sit on a toilet

Auditory
- ☐ Covers ears or screams with sudden loud noises (e.g., vacuum cleaner, toilet flushing)
- ☐ Has difficulty locating sound
- ☐ Enjoys constantly making sounds (e.g., humming)
- ☐ Is constantly distracted by background sounds (e.g., fluorescent lights humming)
- ☐ Prefers music very loud

Vision
- ☐ Demonstrates poor eye contact
- ☐ Turns head to the side when looking at things
- ☐ Holds head very close to work
- ☐ Loses place on page when reading
- ☐ Has difficulty copying from the board
- ☐ Uses hand as a "visor" in bright sunlight or fluorescent lighting
- ☐ Has difficulty tracking a ball to catch

Arousal and Attending
- ☐ Is hyperactive and difficult to calm
- ☐ Has difficulty modulating emotional response
- ☐ Startles easily
- ☐ Is difficult to arouse and does not react to loud sounds, bright lights, etc.
- ☐ Has difficulty completing tasks
- ☐ Has difficulty transitioning from one task to another

Social Consciousness
- ☐ Reacts with laughter when someone expresses anger, sadness, fear
- ☐ Becomes fearful in social situations
- ☐ Does not spontaneously interact in a group
- ☐ Appears to be unaware of others' feelings
- ☐ Unable to identify happy/sad/angry faces

Olfactory/Gustatory
- ☐ Complains of things "smelling bad"
- ☐ Notices how people smell
- ☐ Reacts violently to smells
- ☐ Smells objects constantly
- ☐ Prefers foods that are highly spiced or totally bland
- ☐ Chooses very limited repertoire of foods (e.g., prefers smooth vs. texture)

Too much sensory input from the environment can cause a child's neurological system to overload and can result in physiological stress responses. These responses frequently manifest themselves in fight, flight, or freeze reactions. Sensory overload is also known as "sensory defensiveness" (originally introduced by Knickerbocker in 1980, and later by P. Wilbarger, 1991).

Sensory overload is caused by an excessive amount of sensory input that the child's nervous system inaccurately registers as a threat. When the sensory information is perceived as threatening, the child may overreact to sensations from sights, sounds, or touch, causing disorganized responses to these sensations. This results in an imbalance between inhibition and excitation of the central nervous system. The dance between inhibition and facilitation produces *sensory modulation*, or the ability to regulate reactions to sensory input in an adaptive manner. This can affect attention and behavior. For example, sensory inhibition reduces excessive brain activity by blocking some sensory impulses so that the brain can maintain an appropriate arousal level. Sensory facilitation, on the other hand, increases brain activity by sending information forward and allowing the child to pay attention to pertinent information in the environment. The key is to find a "just right" challenge for each child so that his or her nervous system can properly modulate sensory input, allowing the child to engage in purposeful and meaningful activity.

In the following we will take a closer look at the individual sensory systems. The sensory systems are presented in the order in which neurological development occurs.

iNDiViDUAL SENSORY SYSTEMS

Vestibular System

The vestibular system is made up of structures in the inner ear that detect movement and changes in head position. For example, this system allows us to know the speed at which we are moving, the direction in which we are going such as up or down, backward or forward, or in a circle, and where our body is in space. Basically, the vestibular system may be compared to any slight disturbance of a glass of water. That is, any subtle movement of the head stimulates the vestibular receptors. Linear movement is calming, while rotary movement is more stimulating.

Vestibular information stays in the nervous system for 4-8 hours. This is important to remember when making choices of activities for the group structure. An occupational therapist can inform the educational team about individual children's needs for vestibular input during group activities. Too much vestibular input can cause a child who does not process movement well to experience symptoms of nausea or headaches. Other signs and symptoms of vestibular system dysfunction include gravitational insecurity (fear of heights), difficulty sitting still, a craving for spinning, or avoidance of playground equipment.

Proprioception System

Receptors in our joints, muscles, and tendons perceive contraction, stretching and compression in our body. This allows us to coordinate movements without having to look at each body part while it moves. Proprioceptive input stays in the nervous system for up to 1-1/2 hours. The system may be compared to anything more than just the weight of an extremity, and is also referred to as "heavy work." This includes activities such as lifting, pushing, pulling, tugging, carrying weighted objects, or even receiving a hug or massage.

The sensory input gained from this system can be either alerting or calming. Children who have difficulty registering proprioceptive input accurately may demonstrate lack of coordination, poor articulation, and difficulty grading the amount of pressure needed, such as sitting down very hard or coloring with heavy pressure on a crayon.

Tactile System

Cells in our skin send information about touch, pain, temperature, and pressure to the brain. We have more tactile receptors in the mouth and hands than anywhere else in the body. For example, infants explore their environment by mouthing toys, since they can more easily learn about shape, size, and texture from tactile contact. The tactile system works to protect us in a defensive manner by alerting us to danger such as hot water or the prick of a needle. The tactile system also helps us discriminate and orient to our environment, so that we know that something is touching us, where it is touching us, what type of touch it is, and the attributes of the touch such as texture, size, shape, and temperature. A newborn's tactile system responds with more of a defensive reaction as a survival mechanism. As the child develops and his nervous system matures, the discriminative aspect of the tactile system is more prominent. Light, cold, or rough touch is alerting, whereas heavy, deep, warm, or soft touch is calming. Tactile information stays in the nervous system for up to 1-1/2 hours.

The child who responds to non-noxious tactile input with a protective rather than a discriminative response demonstrates tactile defensiveness. This is a fight, flight or freeze response to harmless tactile stimuli. Children who do not register tactile input accurately may be hypersensitive to typical tactile experiences and therefore avoid particular touch input such as finger painting, glue, or textured surfaces like grass, or they may complain about tags in shirts, discomfort with hair and nail cutting, or even particular types of clothing material. Other children are hyposensitive and may not register enough tactile input to notice and learn, seeking out extra sensory experiences such as mouthing objects past a typical developmental age.

Visual System

Receptors in the retina are stimulated by light and send information to the brain about the visual world around us. The visual system is affected by *acuity*, the focusing mechanism of the eyes; *ocular motor*, the muscles of the eyes that allow us to track a moving object; *visual motor coordination*, which helps us to perform skilled tasks such as catching a ball or handwriting; and *visual perception*, which is the interpretation of visual information in our environment such as detecting subtle differences in faces or finding matching socks.

Children with visual system deficits may exhibit a variety of symptoms – from sensitivity to bright lights to difficulty hitting a baseball. Visual input can have either an alerting or a calming affect on a child. For example, bright lights, bold colors, and highly decorated rooms can be alerting, whereas natural lighting, pastel colors, and uncluttered rooms can be calming.

Auditory System

Receptors in the inner ear are stimulated by airwaves and send sound information to the brain for interpretation. The auditory system allows us to hear, discriminate, and localize sounds. This is important for learning language and communication. Children with a hearing impairment or an auditory processing difficulty may demonstrate delays in speech and language skills.

A child with an auditory processing problem has a normal structural system for hearing, but has difficulty discriminating sounds, remembering what is heard, and organizing auditory input. A child with a hearing impairment, on the other hand, demonstrates hearing loss in sound decibels, ranging from a mild hearing loss at 25-40dB to a profound hearing loss at 95dB or greater. Causes of a hearing impairment include a variety of conditions such as serious otitis, perforation, scarring, middle-ear anomaly, or a sensori-neural complication.

Some children have auditory sensitivity. For example, a child may have difficulty filtering out background sounds and may appear to have an attention problem. Other children are hypersensitive to loud sounds and become distressed even by typical sounds. Thus, they may cover their ears when hearing the sound of a dog barking or a toilet flushing. Quick, loud sound is alerting, whereas slow, rhythmic sound is calming. This is important to remember when choosing songs and music for the children's sensory needs during group activities.

Olfactory System

Chemical receptors are located in the nasal structure and allow us to smell and discriminate between various smells. In addition, direct neuronal connections between the nasal receptors and the limbic system are responsible for emotional memory and also for storing long-term memory. Thus, smell can be a very powerful sensory experience – both pleasant, such as remembering a special holiday with family after whiffing apple pie, or unpleasant, such as remembering an ex-spouse by the smell of a certain cologne or perfume. Smell can be so noxious that it affects a child's feeding and nutritional growth due to avoidance of certain food smells and therefore a limited diet.

Smells that are sweet are calming, such as cinnamon or vanilla, whereas citrus or peppermint scents are more alerting. However, the same scent can have different effects on different people. Some children have an aversive reaction to typically pleasant scents, causing a fight, flight or freeze stress response. While often viewed as not as important as other sensory systems, the olfactory system can have potent input for a child, as it may trigger a positive emotion and therefore entice participation, or trigger a negative emotion and cause a child to avoid a given activity. This is important to keep in mind when planning activities that involve smells.

Gustatory System

Chemical receptors on the tongue allow us to differentiate between flavors such as sweet, sour, salty, or bitter, as well as textures such as soft, hard, sticky, or crunchy. Oral motor input of blowing or sucking can be very organizing for the nervous system. For example, babies learn to comfort themselves by sucking to get nourishment or simply to pacify and calm. Also, babies explore their world by mouthing objects, as they discriminate the size, shape, and texture of an object.

Oral motor input can help to modulate our nervous systems so that we can attain and maintain a "just right" alertness level. For example, if you are feeling fatigued after lunch, chewing on spicy gum or candy can help you to "wake up." Or if you are feeling stressed after a long day at work, sucking a milkshake through a straw can have a calming and organizing effect as it sends neuronal messages to the brain through our cranial nerves. In general, foods that are crunchy, sour, salty, or cold are alerting, whereas warm, sweet, or chewy foods are calming. In addition, activities that include blowing bubbles, whistles, cotton balls, or feathers are not only fun but also help children learn diaphragmatic breathing for sensory organization and calming. Deep breathing can be used as a tool at any time to help a child develop sensory self-regulation skills. In other words, as a child matures, he can learn how to regulate his own sensory system by choosing activities, actions, foods, and so on, that help him attain and maintain a "just right" alertness level throughout his day.

CHAPTER 2

SCHOOL READINESS SKILLS

he early childhood activities in the lessons presented later in this book are designed so that children have fun while at the same learning and improving their sensorimotor skills. This chapter gives an overview of the skills covered in each lesson with particular emphasis on the relevance of the various activities for school readiness.

In each group session the children work on multiple skills, including sensory, gross-/fine-motor, social/emotional, cognitive, language, and oral motor skills. While the sensory and motor skills are the foundation of each lesson, as outlined below, cognitive, language, oral motor, and social/emotional skills are woven into the activities to comprise a more comprehensive whole.

SENSORY SKILLS

Since the vestibular and proprioceptive senses are the first to develop before birth and are the foundation senses for all other skills and learning, they are always introduced in the first activities in each lesson. For example, vestibular input is incorporated through a variety of movement activities – climbing, jumping, and so on. Proprioceptive activities follow the vestibular activities because the deep pressure input is very organizing to the nervous system whereas some types of vestibular input can be over-alerting. The key is to find a balance so that the children are actively engaged and the group as a whole is able to maintain a "just right" alertness level for attending and learning. As the vestibular and proprioceptive senses are stimulated, children may demonstrate an improved ability to know where their body is in space and consequently motor plan new actions.

Throughout each group session, the children are also exposed to a variety of tactile input. For example, if the theme is "Winter Snow," they may walk barefoot through a pile of pretend snow (packing peanuts), and for the fine-motor activity they may create snow sculptures using salty textured play dough. Finally, the senses of taste and smell are stimulated. For example, if the theme is "Holiday Fun," the children may explore the taste of candy canes or use peppermint-scented finger paint. Similarly, if the theme is "Insects," the children may create an "ants on the log" snack consisting of celery, peanut butter, and raisins. Activity choices are limited only by your imagination.

Organized sensory processing as overviewed above helps children attain the following functional school skills:

- Focusing and attending to task
- Writing/coloring with appropriate pencil/crayon pressure
- Standing in line with classmates
- Participating in tactile table activities
- Enjoying all types of food snacks

MOTOR SKILLS

Throughout the group sessions, motor activity plays a major role as a way to strengthen children's muscles, improve coordination, and practice finer manipulative movements, including eye-hand coordination.

Gross-Motor Skills

Gross-motor skills are facilitated during the vestibular and proprioceptive activities and sometimes during an action song or a balance task. Overall strength in the arms, legs, and trunk muscles is gained from repetitive active play. Gross-motor development helps students accomplish the following functional school skills:

- Sitting upright at a desk
- Participating in physical education requirements
- Accessing playground equipment

- Managing stairs
- Balancing on toilet seat
- Maneuvering through the classroom

Fine-Motor Skills

Throughout the lessons, the children work on such fine-motor skills as grip-and-pinch strength for arch development, pincer grasp for dexterity, thumb-and-finger opposition for maintaining an open thumb web space, and in-hand manipulation skills for separation of the two sides of the hand to develop a balance between skill and power. These skills are important for performing the following functional school skills:

- Holding a pencil correctly
- Controlling scissors when cutting
- Manipulating buttons and zippers on clothing
- Tying shoes
- Using a paintbrush
- Turning a doorknob
- Pushing a water fountain button
- Using utensils

Bilateral Coordination Skills

Bilateral coordination skills refer to the ability to use both sides of the body in a coordinated fashion. These skills are addressed during group time to facilitate the development of hand dominance and may require large-muscle involvement in which children cross the midline of their body. Bilateral coordination skills lead to the development of handedness by requiring both hands to be used together in a coordinated fashion. This allows for "hold and do" patterns so that one hand is actively "doing," for example, coloring, while the other hand is "holding" or stabilizing the paper. Repetition gradually allows for an age-appropriate hand dominance to emerge. Some bilateral movements are symmetrical whereas others are asymmetrical (reciprocal or alternating). Mastering these movements is important for students to be successful with the following functional school skills:

- Washing hands
- Climbing stairs by alternating feet
- "Hold and do" tasks such as holding a piece of paper while cutting or coloring it
- Catching a ball
- Clapping hands
- Skipping, hopscotch, or jumping jacks

Eye-Hand Coordination Skills

Eye-hand coordination skills are essential in a child's development for school readiness. Since many school requirements involve handwriting, it is important that children have a solid foundation in visual motor integration. In addition, eye-hand coordination activities help children develop ocular motor skills for tracking when reading and copying from the board. Eye-hand coordination skills help students be successful with the following functional school skills:

- Cutting accurately
- Copying shapes
- Writing the letters of the alphabet
- Assembling puzzles
- Coloring within the lines

SOCIAL/EMOTIONAL SKILLS

Nurturing a child's emotional well-being is the most important aspect of any therapeutic program. Developing a sense of self-confidence is imperative for successful social interaction. Self-concept begins with a child's emotional development. Thus, fostering emotional growth is an integral aspect of the group sessions. For example, every child is repeatedly praised for accomplishing a task, and each achievement inherently reinforces the child's feeling of success. If children have a positive self-concept, they are more likely to succeed at any given task, and they are more motivated to actively engage in group activities, which develops improved self-control. The group activities allow the children to be successful at their own level of ability.

Non-compliant behavior and difficulty attending to task impact a student's availability to learn. In other words, if a child refuses to complete an activity or has trouble following directions, he will miss out on important information for learning. Attending to task and listening to instructions is a primary skill needed for each child to be ready to learn in a school environment. The structure of each lesson plan inherently addresses this throughout the group session. For example, the children are asked to sit on a designated "spot" while listening to instructions between activities. Also, directions are brief and spoken using simple language so the children can easily understand and maintain attention.

Effective social skills are necessary for students to acquire the following functional school skills:

- Cooperating

- Attending to task
- Following the leader
- Taking turns
- Sharing
- Following directions

COGNITIVE SKILLS

Academic pre-readiness skills are taught as the children engage in purposeful activities throughout each group session. Specifically, pre-academic skills are emphasized to help the students achieve success in the following functional school skills:

- Pre-math skills (counting and identifying numbers)
- Letter recognition
- Shape identification
- Color identification
- Visual perceptual skills, such as matching, discrimination, memory
- Position concepts of up/down, under/over, front/back, on/off
- Reasoning and problem-solving skills

LANGUAGE

The group sessions are rich in possibilities for developing and expanding language skills. Speech and language skills occur concurrently with the development of other skills. Communication skills are introduced, modeled, and taught through play; thus, incidental learning occurs. The speech language pathologist models appropriate ways to stimulate speech, language, and articulation skills to any children with speech/language delays during group time so that other staff members can observe and learn. This transdisciplinary approach allows for role delineation so that, for example, when the speech language pathologist is absent, the classroom teacher or other trained professionals can assist the children with production of clear articulation and age-appropriate language skills. Speech and language skills are necessary to help students develop the following functional school skills:

- Receptive communication for understanding instructions
- Following 1- to 2-step directions

- Expressive communication (vocalizations for sequencing sounds into words)
- Non-verbal communication such as gestures and sign language
- Vocabulary skills

ORAL MOTOR SKILLS

The lessons also help children develop oral motor skills for clear articulation as well as feeding skills. Oral motor skills are incorporated within a variety of activities using multiple stimuli, thereby promoting more opportunity for carryover, generalization, and motor learning.

Oral motor skills develop through input from multiple sensory motor modalities involving visual, tactile, auditory, gustatory, vestibular, and proprioception. Oral motor movements are learned through repetition and feedback until motor planning sequences develop. These skills are necessary for students to acquire the following functional school skills:

- Chewing food
- Sucking through a straw
- Safe swallowing
- Clear speech
- Blowing instruments

CHAPTER 3

PROGRAM STRUCTURE

his chapter will discuss the basic structure and format of the thematic group sessions that make up the core of this book by describing the seven components that comprise each lesson plan. Activity examples are also included.

The seven components are arranged in a developmental sensory sequence to stimulate the basic sensory systems prior to introducing the higher-level skills of balance, eye-hand coordination, and fine-motor skills. In addition, as mentioned, the vestibular activity in each lesson precedes the proprioceptive activity because firm-pressure touch is very organizing to the nervous system after a movement task.

OVERVIEW OF LESSON COMPONENTS

Each lesson in *Learn to Move, Move to Learn!* is organized in a sensory integrative developmental sequence consisting of seven activities that all relate to the selected theme. Each session takes 45-60 minutes.

Have the children begin each session by sitting on the floor in a circle. It is recommended that the children sit in a designated spot they are familiar with from their daily classroom activities. Always verbally instruct, visually demonstrate, and physically model for the children prior to each activity so that they have multiple opportunities to understand the directions using different modalities.

The following sequence makes up each lesson plan:

1. Warm-Up
2. Vestibular
3. Proprioception
4. Balance
5. Eye-Hand Coordination
6. Cool-Down
7. Fine Motor

Warm-Up

The purpose of the warm-up is to cue the children that group time is about to begin and to introduce the theme for the day. When choosing your own warm-up activity, remember to always relate it to the theme. Every lesson plan includes reading a storybook. Sometimes it is used as the warm-up; at other times, it is used as the cool-down. A storybook is chosen as the warm-up only when all the activities in the lesson plan reflect the storybook directly. For example, in the book *Pete's a Pizza*, a young boy is sad that he cannot go outside to play because it is raining. His dad helps cheer him up by making Pete into a pretend pizza. Consistent with the theme, the children engage in activities pretending to make each other into pizzas, and each component of the lesson includes an activity related to the storyline in the book. Here are a few general examples of warm-up activities:

- Simple songs
- Finger plays
- Action songs
- Storybook reading

Vestibular

Because too much movement can be overstimulating to some children, activities in this category are only repeated a few times. Also, if the task requires rotating vestibular input, be sure the children move in both directions in order to balance the vestibular system. Again, the activity is directly related to the theme of the lesson. For example, if the theme is "Pumpkins," the children take turns pretending to be a pumpkin, hugging their knees while rolling back and forth on a mat. Here are a few general examples of activities:

- Rolling on a mat side to side, with knees tucked; over pillows
- Spinning while standing

- Locomotor tasks: gallop, run, hop, skip, jump, crab walk, bear walk
- Scooter board relays
- Obstacle course

Proprioception

Next, the children participate in a "heavy work" activity (see page 6) to stimulate their proprioceptive system. This may involve carrying, lifting, passing, pushing, or pulling resistive objects. (*Note: Because stimulation of the proprioception system is very organizing to the nervous system, give the children several turns with this type of activity.*) Again, the activity is related to the theme. For example, if the theme is "Apples," the children may pass a basket of heavy apples around a circle while music is playing. Here are a few general examples:

- Lifting and carrying heavy objects
- Passing a heavy object around a circle of kids
- Pushing and pulling heavy objects
- Using a beanbag chair to make a kid into a "sandwich"
- Jumping on a mini-trampoline
- Theraband stretching

Balance

Balance activities are introduced next because they require the foundation of an integrated vestibular and proprioception system, which has been established by now. That is, if a child knows where her body is in space in relation to objects and people, has good postural stability, and can spontaneously execute righting reactions, she will be more successful with higher-level balance tasks. Again, the activity in this component of the lesson is related to the theme. For example, if the theme is "Shapes," the children may balance while walking on circles of hula-hoops that are placed on the floor or jump ropes that are formed into squares. Here are a few general examples:

- Balance beam; walk forward, backward, sideways; stoop to pick up object
- Walking on hula-hoop, jump rope, or strip of tape on the floor
- Playing balance games (e.g., "Simon says stand on one foot")
- Kid yoga balance poses
- Balance boards

Eye-Hand Coordination

Integrated eye-hand coordination is essential for success at school and later life. Specifically, eye-hand coordination allows a child to master purposeful activities such as accurately cutting on a line, stringing beads, catching a ball, and reproducing shapes, numbers, and letters. Since eye-hand coordination involves high levels of skill, the activity may need to be graded for each child's ability. For example, a child who has difficulty catching may need to use a large-sized ball, or a balloon as it moves slower than a ball, thus allowing more time for the child to catch. Again, the activity relates to the lesson theme. Thus, when using the theme "Summer Fun," the children might volley a beach ball to a partner. Here are a few general examples:

- Throwing and catching
- Using balls, beanbags, balloons, bubbles
- Throwing in a bucket, at a target, to a friend

Cool-Down

The cool-down time helps the children attain a "just right" alertness level in preparation for the fine-motor task to follow. A storybook about the selected theme is often chosen as a cool-down activity, because the children are better able to attend and listen to a book since they just completed a sequence of sensorimotor activities and their nervous systems are now more organized. However, if a storybook was chosen as the warm-up, the children may engage in a relaxation activity or sing a song related to the theme for the cool-down activity. For example, in the theme "Winter Snow," the children can pretend to be snowmen melting by slowly lowering themselves from standing to lying down on the floor. Here are a few general examples for a cool-down activity:

- Relaxation activity
- Simple songs
- Finger plays
- Reading a storybook (see above)

Fine Motor

After the cool-down, the children transition one at a time to a table for the fine-motor task. On occasion, the fine-motor task is completed while the children are prone (on their tummy) on the floor. For example, if the fine-motor activity was a group project using large bulletin board paper to color a field of flowers, it would work best to have the children complete this task on the floor.

A variety of adaptations may be used for children with delayed fine-motor skills. For example, if a child cannot squeeze a glue bottle, he can use a glue stick instead. A child can work on developing a correct pencil grasp by holding a Q-tip and dipping it into a pool of glue.

As always, the fine-motor activity must be related to the theme. For example, for the theme "Circus," the children can make paper plate clown faces by drawing a face on the plate and gluing yarn for hair, finally adding a triangle hat. Here are a few general examples of fine-motor activities:

- Art with focus on the process
- Making a snack
- Cutting and gluing
- Coloring
- Drawing
- Tactile activity

Since many preschool children have not yet learned how to write their names, they are taught to practice drawing pre-writing shapes on their art projects. The leader tells them, *"write your name on your paper,"* and shows the children how to reproduce shapes in the developmental sequence of a circle, a plus, and a square. Children with very delayed visual motor integration skills can trace the shapes or imitate drawing the shapes.

Transitions

Transitions are difficult for some children with sensory processing problems because changes in routine can cause a stress response that leads to a fight, flight, or freeze reaction. To prevent this outcome, the children regroup after each activity by sitting back in a circle on their designated spots. Monitor the group's activity level and decide whether to discontinue an activity or move on to the next, depending on the behavioral response of the group as a whole. For example, if the children are engaged in a parachute activity and the noise level increases, the children may become overly excited and fail to follow simple directions. In such cases, the adult facilitator may choose to have the children sit down while holding the parachute, attempt to calm the children by talking in a whisper and moving the parachute slowly, or discontinue the activity. Also, deep breathing and firm-pressure touch are organizing and can have a modulating effect on the nervous system. That is, it can provide a calming effect for the child who is excitable, and an alerting affect on the child who is lethargic.

The children perform the following transition routine at the beginning of group time and between each activity as needed. The children imitate the teacher leader after each step.

1. Demonstrate wrapping your arms around yourself and squeezing firmly. Then say, "Give yourself a hug."
2. Next, interlock your fingers and place them on top of your head. Then say, "Push on your head."
3. Have each child hold a small feather in the palms of his or her hands. Demonstrate taking a deep breath and then gently blowing the feather so that it stays in your hands. Say, "Blow a feather; don't let it fall." (This is an excellent way to teach children diaphragmatic breathing as it gives tactile and visual feedback.)
4. Touch all of your fingers together with your thumb to form a hand puppet. Say, "Kiss your brain," then kiss the mouth of the hand puppet and touch it to the top of your head.
5. Now say, "You're so smart; you're ready to start!"

In conclusion, the sequence of seven activities that make up each group session is designed to stimulate the foundation sensory systems, while facilitating the development of coordination required for successful school readiness skills.

CHAPTER 4

ADAPTATIONS

o ensure that the lesson plans outlined later in this book will have maximum benefit for the broadest range of children with varying skill and ability levels, this chapter will discuss how to adapt tasks to meet each child's needs. Specifically, we will look at the use of adaptive equipment and materials to assist with functional independence for group participation, special considerations for a variety of disabilities, including autism spectrum disorders, cerebral palsy, Down Syndrome, visual impairment, hearing impairment, and other exceptionalities. Also, use of music, play, and adult interaction to facilitate best practice techniques in assisting children with special needs will be addressed.

TASK ANALYSIS: "JUST RIGHT" CHALLENGE

A variety of adaptations may be necessary for each child's success with a given activity. It is important to analyze a task step-by-step, and allow each child to participate at his or her ability level in order to achieve a "just right" challenge. This check should be performed during each group session, for every task, and for any child with special needs. To illustrate, if the task is to throw a beanbag into a bucket, the steps might look something like this:

1. Stand on a place marker holding a beanbag.
2. Look at a bucket about 5 feet away.
3. Move arm in an underswing pattern.
4. Toss the beanbag toward the bucket.

5. Release the ball from hand.

6. Make a basket!

A child with severe physical impairments may be working on simply releasing objects. Thus, the bucket would be placed in close proximity to the child's body, and a beanbag would be placed in her hand. Then the child would be encouraged to open her hand and drop the beanbag into the bucket. In short, this child would begin her "just right" challenge at Step #5. Similarly, a child with developmental delays and difficulty with eye-hand coordination may simply need the bucket placed closer. This child would begin his "just right" challenge with an adaptation at Step #2, and the bucket would be placed 2 feet away instead of 5 feet away.

ADAPTIVE EQUIPMENT AND MATERIALS

Some children require special adaptive equipment in order to be able to participate in a given activity. For example, a child who is unable to independently use regular scissors for cutting paper could use adaptive scissors such as loop scissors that only require squeezing. Or a child with severe physical impairments may need an adaptive scooter board for positioning and safety during scooter board activities.

Materials may also be adapted. For example, using a larger-sized ball would help children with poor catching skills attain a "just right" challenge. Or a child with poor balance could walk across a piece of tape on the floor rather than a balance beam.

SPECIAL CONSIDERATIONS

Countless adaptations are possible for each task, dependent upon the individual child's motor, cognitive, and language needs. It is left to the discretion of the reader to make professional decisions regarding adaptations necessary for "just right" challenges for each group session. Some general special considerations are included in this book for children with autism spectrum disorders, cerebral palsy, Down Syndrome, hearing impairment, visual impairment, and other exceptionalities. These diagnoses were chosen, as they are the ones most commonly seen in my practice.

Autism Spectrum Disorders

Children with an autism spectrum disorder have multiple sensory processing needs.

Therefore, these children benefit from increased proprioceptive input throughout each group session as this helps to organize the nervous system for calming and focusing. For example, allowing more turns for the proprioception activity is beneficial. In addition, it is helpful to provide a weighted lap bag for the child to use during seated circle time. Or, if the child tolerates touch, a trained adult can apply joint compression to the child's limbs and trunk. The adult may be a paraprofessional, teacher, or therapist; however, it is important that an occupational or physical therapist provide the initial training and monitor for correct technique so that the joints are protected from damage.

Cerebral Palsy

Some children with cerebral palsy (CP) have very limited mobility. Thus, an occupational or physical therapist may need to use special handling and positioning techniques to allow these children to be able to fully participate in an activity. An occupational or physical therapist can train and monitor others on proper handling techniques to use when transferring a child with limited mobility from one position to another. Once the therapists feel confident that the other professionals are competent at appropriately handling the child with CP, role delineation can occur and the transdisciplinary approach is put into practice.

Also, many tasks will need to be simplified to allow children with CP to be independent as they complete tasks – an important consideration given that it is a basic human right to feel empowered by doing things independently. For example, a child with limited movement may have a goal to simply grasp and release an object. Thus, for a beanbag toss activity, the child would be expected to grasp the beanbag and release it into a bucket that is positioned in close proximity. Further, using a communication device during group time can encourage participation and independence for children with CP who are nonverbal. For example, a switch-activated device can be prerecorded to say, *"You're so smart, you're ready to start!"* – the last step of the transition routine.

Down Syndrome

For children with Down Syndrome, extra precaution must be taken to avoid spinal cord injury. A condition known as atlantoaxial instability, which is a combination of hypotonia (low muscle tone), ligament laxity, and odontoid maldevelopment (protruding boney process) of C-1 C-2 spinal articulations, can only be diagnosed by an x-ray usually after age 4. Only about 10%-20% of the children with Down Syndrome have this condition; however, it is best to apply contra-indications to all children with Down Syndrome.

These include avoiding any activity that causes the neck to move into extreme flexion or extension, such as tumbling, jumping on trampolines, doing somersaults, riding on roller coasters, and engaging in contact sports.

Hearing Impairment

Using simple sign language when giving directions for an activity allows the child with a hearing impairment to better understand how to perform the activity. It is also useful for the other children to be exposed to sign language, so that they can communicate with their friend who has the hearing impairment. In addition, visual cue cards can be used for tasks that are repeated in several of the lesson plans. For example, a black-and-white outline picture of a balloon may be shown to the children prior to a balloon volley activity.

The same approach may be used for log rolling, bear walking, beanbag toss, obstacle course, or any number of repeated activities. In addition, as the children engage in each task, the child with the hearing impairment can observe and imitate; giving this child more time to process directions ensures more independent participation in group activities.

Visual Impairment

Verbal prompts with simple instructions help a child with a visual impairment to better understand directions for an activity. Using one hand slightly touching underneath the child's arm or hand to guide her through an obstacle course will ensure more independent participation. Some obstacles may be too difficult and unsafe for the child with a visual impairment, such as a balance beam; a path made of tape on the floor can be used as an adaptation.

High-contrast materials with tactile feedback can assist a child with a visual impairment to participate more successfully in group activities. For example, a black outline made with a dried glue boundary on a coloring page allows a child to feel the edge of the picture with the crayon and, therefore, be more likely to color within the lines.

Other Exceptionalities

Some children are identified as having delays in development in their early childhood years; however, the cause of the delays is often unclear. Some of these children receive an educational label of learning disability, behavior disorder, or other health impaired after they have entered elementary school.

Children with such developmental delays often have difficulty with basic learning skills such as identifying colors, numbers, and letters. The lesson plans are designed to repeat many of these cognitive skills, allowing these children to be more successful at remembering basic concepts for school readiness skills. In addition, due to the structure of the group sessions, children with behavior difficulties, for example, develop coping skills for learning how to share, waiting for their turn, and complying with instructions.

TiME-LiMiTED SESSiON

Another adaptation to consider is a time-limited session. Generally, individual group sessions last between 45-60 minutes. However, if you have only 30 minutes, it is recommended that the children engage in the following program sequence:

1. Warm-Up (song or finger play)
2. Proprioception
3. Cool-Down (book)
4. Fine Motor

If time is an issue, it is best to follow this sequence because the warm-up introduces the children to the theme, the proprioceptive task involves them in a sensory organizing activity, followed by emergent literacy exposure and fine-motor skill development for school readiness. However, this type session is not as effective as using the entire program structure because it does not stimulate all of the sensory systems in an integrated manner. As mentioned earlier, when all of the sensory systems are integrated and working smoothly, the child's nervous system is ready for learning.

One way to create time for a full session is for the group to meet every other week for 60 minutes instead of 30 minutes every week. Be sure the parents are informed of how services will be carried out for their child, and write a statement describing this service delivery in the child's individualized education program (IEP).

ADDiTiONAL THERAPEUTiC TOOLS

Learning should be FUN! Play is an integral aspect of a child's development. As children engage in pretend play, they are engrossed in a world of their own, unaware that they are, in fact, working hard to develop and improve motor, cognitive, language, and social skills.

The use of rhythm and music are additional tools that enhance a child's ability to develop these skills. For example, music can enrich group sessions by helping children learn language, build self-esteem, and experience a sense of belonging with their friends. Consulting a music therapist on creative ideas would be helpful. Children are also learning cooperation, sharing, and turn taking during the group activities, essential social skills for school readiness.

In addition, "therapeutic use of self" is a crucial tool that must be carefully used by the adults. This concept is about each adult's personal awareness and his or her ability to monitor and adjust voice tone, body language, and interactions to each child's unique and special needs. This allows for optimal interactions between the professional team members as well as the children.

This chapter has reviewed suggestions for modifying activities and materials for children with a variety of diagnoses. All children can participate in the group activities at any level of ability with only a few adaptations for a successful and enjoyable experience!

CHAPTER 5

DYNAMIC PROBLEM SOLVING

f it doesn't work, it's evaluation. If it works, it's therapy!" As creative practitioners, we are challenged to utilize best practice techniques through a continuous discovery of trial and error. It is imperative that we always keep an open mind and learn the art of flexibility! This chapter discusses how to collaborate with a team of professionals during a group session, offers suggestions for choosing a facilitator, and provides examples of creative ways to maintain compliance from the class as a whole.

COLLABORATION

On-site collaboration is the key to helping each child attain success with every task. The collaborative effort of the occupational therapist (OT), physical therapist (PT), speech language pathologist (SLP), early childhood teacher, paraeducator, and others provides an atmosphere of adult cooperation. This is an excellent model for the children to learn from as well!

This collaborative effort starts during planning and continues throughout the group session. For example, if the teacher observes a child having difficulty with a balance task and communicates this to the PT, together they can find a solution to help the child be successful. Similarly, if the SLP observes a child having difficulty cutting paper and communicates this to the OT, the OT can show the SLP how to best help that child cut with better accuracy. And if the paraeducator hears a child articulating the letter "f" incorrectly, for example, and communicates this to the SLP, the SLP can show the paraeducator how to assist the child with correct pronunciation. The beauty of a transdisciplinary approach is that all of the adults learn from each other and can carry out therapeutic techniques in all areas, thus truly working with the whole child.

Another collaborative effort involves placing the equipment to "fit" the classroom space. Deciphering where to position each piece of equipment is important, since every classroom is set up differently. In addition, the team needs to decide who is going to set up the equipment and who will be supervising the children. For example, if the teacher leader reads the storybook, some of the other adults can sit with the children at the circle and help a child who may have behavior difficulties, while yet others prepare for the fine-motor activity coming up later on.

Given a relatively tight schedule, it is helpful if the adults are organized so that the transitions from one activity to another are smooth. This also helps keep the children on track. Thus, it is recommended that materials be prepared prior to the start of each session. Please note that it takes several sessions for both the children and the adults to become familiar with the routine and that early sessions, therefore, take longer.

LEADERSHIP ROLES

There are several ways to decide how to assign the leadership responsibility for a group session. The most effective way is to assign one adult to lead the whole session. This helps the children know who to focus their attention on for the "teacher." It also allows one adult to facilitate the group activities while the other adults assist individual children. The facilitator can be the same person every session, such as the OT, or can vary from one session to the next. For example, one time the PT may lead the group session, the next time the SLP, and so on.

Another way of distributing leadership and responsibility involves assigning a different adult professional to lead one or two of the activities in the sequence. For example, the SLP may lead the warm-up by reading a book and then facilitate language skills by asking questions about the book. The OT may lead the vestibular and proprioception activities, the PT may lead the balance and eye-hand coordination activities, and finally the classroom teacher may lead the cool-down and fine-motor activities.

Note: The group sessions may be implemented with any combination of adult professionals, but there must always be an OT or a PT present who is trained in sensory integration in order to ensure the safety of the children.

MONITORING AND ADJUSTING GROUP ACTIVITY LEVELS

All the lesson plans in this book have been field-tested and refined over the years so that they allow for ease with transitions as well as optimal therapeutic interventions. However, every classroom is comprised of a unique combination of personalities and abilities. Therefore, it will be necessary to adjust an activity to meet the unique needs of your group of children. Adjusting an activity for a "just right" challenge not only applies to each child as mentioned in the Adaptations chapter, but also to the group as a whole.

It takes experience and insightful observations to monitor the group activity level and subsequently regulate therapeutic interaction and guidance to help the group attain a "just right" alertness level. For example, if the children are engaged in a spinning activity for vestibular input and become overly excitable, (a) the teacher leader would moderate the activity so that the children spin more slowly, (b) the teacher would lead the children through the transition sequence (see Transitions, page 22) for deep-pressure touch to organize and calm the children, or (c) the activity would be stopped and the children go on to the next activity.

As illustrated, team work is essential to ensure that activities are planned well and the lessons are carried out smoothly and efficiently. The consistency and structure inherent in a well-planned lesson not only make the activities go better but also support the children so they are better able to perform at their maximum ability level.

CHAPTER 6

PLANNING

he thematic group lesson plans in this book are based on a synthesis of creative ideas generated by a combination of original inventions, ideas gained from workshops and conferences, consulting websites, and reviewing activity books (see References/Bibliography and Suggested Readings as well as Resources) over years of trial and error, and with input and suggestions from multiple professionals.

This chapter discusses ways to meet individual student goals through the activities and offers suggestions for documentation. In addition, ideas are presented for equipment and materials that may be used for group activities. Finally, readers will learn how to create their own lesson plans

FUNCTIONAL OUTCOMES AND GOALS

The lesson plans cover a broad range of skills, including the school readiness skills discussed in Chapter 2. Activities in each lesson plan must address the IEP goals for every child with special needs. When planning for your students, review the goals listed in each child's IEP and tweak a proposed activity accordingly. For example, in the theme "Spring Flowers," the children cut a small piece of paper in half to make two flower stems. If a child's goal is snipping with scissors, he or she can snip the paper to make "grass" instead of cutting on a line, and the teacher can have two stems already cut for the child to glue. Similarly, if the child's IEP goal is to identify colors, the teacher can facilitate this by asking the child, "What color is your painted flower?" If the child's goal is to articulate the letter "f," the teacher may ask the child to say the word "flower" repeatedly.

In order to chart improvement of individual student goals, progress needs to be documented. Almost any format will work so long as data are recorded consistently and carefully. One way involves completing individual data sheets for each child as illustrated below (a reproducible copy is provided in the Appendix, page 152).

Progress Data Collection Form

Child: _____

Goals	Quarterly Date			
	First Quarter	Second Quarter	Third Quarter	Fourth Quarter
1)				
2)				
3)				
4)				
5)				
6)				
7)				
8)				
9)				
10)				
11)				
12)				
13)				
14)				
15)				
16)				
17)				
18)				
19)				
20)				

In this case, the child's name is recorded at the top of the page, with the child's goals written down the left margin.

Another option would be to use a general data sheet to record each skill for all of the children as in the example on the following page (a reproducible copy is provided in the Appendix, page 153). Here a sequence of cutting skills is written at the top of the page and each child's name written down the left margin. As a child accomplishes each individual step or benchmark for cutting, an X can mark the square. Be sure to include the date of accomplishment. This type of chart can be made for a variety of tasks, including one for each area of development.

EQUIPMENT AND MATERIALS

Each lesson plan includes a list of the equipment and materials needed for all of the activities. Most of the equipment and materials recommended are common to early childhood classrooms, allowing teams to begin using the lesson plan activities immediately and at low cost. If you do not have access to one or more of the recommended equipment and materials, you can easily substitute another similar object. For example, in place of stepping stones, small carpet squares may be used. Or in place of hula-hoops, pliable plastic tubing obtained from a hardware store can be made into a circle by wrapping tape around the circumference. Another example is using a 2x4' board to serve as a balance beam.

If you prefer to purchase prefabricated items, you may consult the list of companies provided in the Resources section. Finally, if you have access to an elementary school, you could ask to borrow some of the items from the physical education department.

The following is a list of prefabricated equipment used throughout the lessons:
- Stepping stones
- Hula-hoops
- Therapy balls
- Mats
- Scooter boards
- Parachute
- Balance boards
- Beanbag chairs
- Playground balls
- Jump ropes
- Balance beam
- Beanbags

Progress Data Collection Form

Skill: Cutting

Children	Hold Scissors Date	Hold Scissors Met	Open/Close Scissors Date	Open/Close Scissors Met	Snip Paper Date	Snip Paper Met	Cut Forward Date	Cut Forward Met	Cut Straight Line Date	Cut Straight Line Met	Cut Curved Line Date	Cut Curved Line Met	Cut Simple Shape Date	Cut Simple Shape Met
1) Billy Bob	12/1	X												
2) Milo Carson														
3) Newton Isaac	12/1	X												
4) Norman Jackson	11/4	X												
5) Theresa Kendall														
6) Suzie Lannings														
7) Sarah Michel	12/3	X												
8) Tyler O'Connel	12/3	X												
9) Iyesha Quincy														
10) Gordan Smith	12/4	X												
11)														
12)														
13)														
14)														
15)														
16)														
17)														
18)														
19)														
20)														

The following is a list of low-cost materials and supplies commonly used:

- Scissors, glue, paint
- Balloons or latex-free medical gloves (the latter are increasingly being used instead of balloons for children who are allergic to latex)
- Crepe paper streamers, ribbons
- Theraband
- Boxes
- Books
- Music tapes and compact discs
- Snacks

DELEGATING RESPONSIBILITY AND TEAM WORK

Once the team decides what lesson plan to implement and what materials are required, it is helpful to delegate responsibility for obtaining each item. For example, the classroom teacher may prepare the supplies needed for the fine-motor project. The SLP may find an appropriate book for the theme, or use the book recommended here, and prepare ahead of time by reading through the book and deciding what questions to ask the children. Finally, the OT and PT may coordinate gathering the large equipment needed such as therapy balls, balance beam, scooter boards, tumbling mat, and so on. When the team is organized, the groups run more smoothly and the children do better.

CREATING LESSON PLANS

Creating your own lesson plan can be fun, but it requires time and cooperation. It is best if the entire team meets to brainstorm ideas from all areas of development. This can be done with any frequency, depending on your team's schedule. For example, you can meet once every quarter and plan for three months at a time. Or you can meet more often and plan for a single week. Review the children's goals and be sure to address them in your choice of activities. It takes 15-30 minutes to produce one lesson plan.

There are two options for creating your own lesson plan. The first is to use the outline on page 38 (a reproducible copy is provided in the Appendix, page 154) and create a new theme using original ideas. Be sure each category activity relates to the theme. Choose a book with simple, repeated or rhyming phrases and colorful illustrations. Be creative, and enjoy generating original ideas!

Lesson Plans

Theme:_____

Lesson Plan (Quick View)

1. Warm-Up: _____

2. Vestibular:_____

3. Proprioception: _____

4. Balance: _____

5. Eye-Hand Coordination: _____

6. Cool-Down: _____

7. Fine Motor: _____

Details/Notes

Materials	**Who's Responsible?**
☐ _____	_____
☐ _____	_____
☐ _____	_____
☐ _____	_____
☐ _____	_____
☐ _____	_____
☐ _____	_____
☐ _____	_____
☐ _____	_____
☐ _____	_____

Remember to pay attention to how the activities connect for ease in transitions. This includes putting down and picking up large equipment items, deciding where the children are going to sit for the next task, and being aware of sensory qualities of the combination of chosen activities. The outline includes space to write materials and supplies needed, as well as who is responsible for gathering each item.

A second option for creating lesson plans is to use a lesson plan provided in this book and simply modify some of the activities. The lesson plans have been field-tested for over 13 years, and many hours have been put into refining them. Each lesson plan began very differently than the final version printed here. In other words, certain activities did not go well together due to the nature of equipment placement, type of sensory input, and/or need for reduced number of transitions.

It is helpful to write down the "Quick View" lesson plan outline on a 3x5" index card so that you can refer to the sequence of activities during the group session.

It is with great pleasure that I share this program with you! I truly feel that the children with whom you work with will greatly benefit from the program and develop the skills they need to be successful and lead happy, fulfilling lives.

LESSON THEMES

THEME: ABC'S

LESSON PLAN (QUICK VIEW)

1. **Warm-Up:** The alphabet song (Optional: Use sign language too!)
2. **Vestibular:** Obstacle course (stepping stones, tunnel, mat, with letters)
3. **Proprioception:** Therapy ball "squish the letters"
4. **Balance:** Balance beam letter matching
5. **Eye-Hand Coordination:** Parachute with letters
6. **Cool-Down:** Book: *Eating the Alphabet* by Lois Ehlert
7. **Fine Motor:** Kool-aid play dough letter shapes

1. WARM-UP

Have the children gather in a circle and sing the familiar alphabet song. (Optional: Use the sing language symbols for each of the letters while singing.)

2. VESTIBULAR

Set up an obstacle course using a variety of equipment such as a tunnel to crawl through, stepping stones to walk on, and a mat to roll across. Place alphabet letters along the path, and as the children move through the obstacle course, ask each one in turn to identify a letter or two. Emphasize prepositions to help the children learn word association with whole body movement, such as over, under, around, etc.

3. PROPRIOCEPTION

With the children lying of the floor, show them how to form letters using their bodies. For example, to make a letter "t," have the children lie face-down with arms out to their side at a 90-degree angle from their straight body. Now, using a large therapy ball, "squish" the letter by rolling the ball over the children. Use "just right" firm pressure and see if it calms the children.

4. BALANCE

Set up a balance beam. Give each child a letter and place matching letters at the end of the balance beam on the floor. Have the children walk across the balance beam each holding their own letter. When they reach the end of the beam, they have to find the matching letter. Repeat with a new letter.

5. EYE-HAND COORDINATION

Have all the children grasp a handle on a parachute. Place plastic or paper alphabet letters in the center of the parachute. Instruct the children to move the parachute in a variety of ways such as up and down, around, etc. Have the children keep their eyes on the letters. Ask then to look with their eyes and find the letter____.

6. COOL-DOWN

Read a book about the alphabet. One example is *Eating the Alphabet* by Lois Ehlert (Scholastic, 1989). Discuss the letters of the alphabet along with the foods described in the book.

7. FINE MOTOR

Make the play dough recipe ahead of time or demonstrate how to make it in front of the children.

Recipe
1 cup of flour
1/2 cup of salt
1 package unsweetened Kool-aid
3 tablespoons of oil
1 cup boiling water
Mix flour, oil, salt and Kool-aid in bowl. Add water. Stir and knead.
(Be sure the dough has cooled before the children play with it.)

Encourage the children to play with the dough-pinching, pulling, kneading, and finally rolling it into a snake. Then give each child a paper plate with a large-sized letter drawn on it and have the children form the "snake" dough over the letter. Repeat for several letters.

Materials*
- Tunnel
- Stepping stones
- Mat
- Paper or plastic letters of the alphabet
- 1-2 large therapy balls (beanbag chairs may be substituted)
- Balance beam
- Parachute
- *Eating the Alphabet* by Lois Ehlert (Scholastic, 1989)
- Play dough ingredients (see recipe above)
- Large bowl and spoon for mixing
- Measuring cups and measuring spoons

Here and throughout, the materials are listed in the order needed for lesson activities.

THEME: APPLES

LESSON PLAN (QUICK VIEW)

1. **Warm-Up:** Song: "Apples Are Falling"
2. **Vestibular:** Tumbling "apples" on mat
3. **Proprioception:** Riding scooter board to get apples
4. **Balance:** "Apple tree" balance game
5. **Eye-Hand Coordination:** Parachute with paper apples
6. **Cool-Down:** Book: *Big Red Apple* by Tony Johnston
7. **Fine Motor:** Hand-print apple trees

1. WARM-UP

Teach the children to sing the following song.
"Apples Are Falling"
Sung to: "Are you Sleeping?"
(From preschooleducation.com; original author unknown. Used with permission.)

Apples are falling, apples are falling
(Move arms from above head to ground, wiggle fingers)
From the tree, from the tree. *(Stretch arms up high & wide for tree branches)*
Pick up all the apples, pick up all the apples,
(Pretend to pick apples off the floor)
One, two, three; one, two, three. *(Use fingers to count out 1, 2, 3)*

2. VESTIBULAR

Have the children pretend to be a tumbling apple. Show them how to pretend to be an "apple" by hugging their knees to their chest and rolling back and forth. They can all participate at the same time. Be sure they have plenty of space.

3. PROPRIOCEPTION

Divide the children into 2-3 groups. Tell the children that the scooter boards are pretend cars and they have to go to the store to buy apples. Place a basket of real apples at one end of the room for each group.
Using a variety of apples with different colors, have the children name the color of the apple they "bought." Include at least one apple per child. Have one child from each group move on the scooter board to get an apple and bring it back to their group. Repeat for several turns.

4. BALANCE

While the children are standing on their circle spots, have them pretend to be apple trees by balancing on one leg while stretching their arms out wide. Repeat several times on each foot. Have the children pretend that their fingers each have an apple on it and have them practice counting.

5. EYE-HAND COORDINATION

Have all of the children grasp a handle on the parachute. Place paper apples in the middle of the parachute and have the children gently move the parachute up and down and watch the apples roll around. (Paper apples may be made by crumbling red, green, or yellow copy paper into a ball shape.) Next, have the children walk around in a circle in one direction and then in the other while keeping their eyes on the apples.

6. COOL-DOWN

Read a book about apples. One example is *Big Red Apple* by Tony Johnston, illustrated by Judith Hoffman Corwin (Scholastic, 1999). Discuss how apples grow on trees, different colors of apples, and what foods are made from apples (e.g., applesauce, apple pie).

7. FINE MOTOR

Before the children begin, have them write their shape "name" (circle, plus, square) on a piece of white construction paper. To begin, have the children use brown tempera paint and paint one hand with a paintbrush, then make a handprint on their paper. Provide a wet paper towel so the children can immediately wash their hands. Next, have the children dip a Q-tip into red paint and then create apples on their "handprint" tree.

Materials
- 2-3 scooter boards
- 2-3 baskets
- Apples of different colors – 1 for each child
- Parachute
- Paper apples (crumble red, green, or yellow copy paper into a ball shape)
- *Big Red Apple* by Tony Johnston, illustrated by Judith Hoffman Corwin (Scholastic, 1999)
- White construction paper – 1 sheet for each child
- Paintbrushes
- Brown and red tempera paint
- Wet paper towels
- Q-tips

THEME: CATERPILLARS/ BUTTERFLIES

LESSON PLAN (QUICK VIEW)

1. **Warm-Up: Book:** *The Caterpillow Fight* by Sam McBratney
2. **Vestibular:** Human caterpillar
3. **Proprioception:** Cater"pillow" fight
4. **Balance Beam:** Pretend butterfly on balance beam
5. **Eye-Hand Coordination:** Caterpillar bowling
6. **Cool-Down:** Caterpillar song
7. **Fine Motor:** Coffee filter/clothespin butterfly

1. WARM-UP

Read the book *The Caterpillow Fight* by Sam McBratney, illustrated by Jill Barton (Candlewick Press/Scholastic, 1996). The activities in this lesson plan relate directly to the story of the book. Discuss how caterpillars change into butterflies.

2. VESTIBULAR

Have the children create a human caterpillar.* They first form a line, then assume hands-and-knees position, and grasp the ankles of the child in front of them. The children crawl around the room as a whole caterpillar, continuing to hold onto the ankles of the child in front.

3. PROPRIOCEPTION

Fill several pillowcases with beanbags. Have the children take turns pretending to have a cater"pillow" fight by swinging the pillowcases and hitting the floor. Be sure that the children who are waiting for their turn sit away from the swinging pillowcases for safety.

4. BALANCE

Set up a balance beam in the middle of the room. Give each child 2 colorful streamers. Explain to the children how a caterpillar turns into a butterfly. Now have the children pretend to be a butterfly by walking on the balance beam and waving the streamers as pretend wings.

5. EYE-HAND COORDINATION

Set up 3 bowling pins with a picture of a butterfly on each. Do this in 2 places in the room to allow less waiting time for children to take turns. Explain to the children that the ball is a pretend caterpillar. They are going to roll the ball "caterpillar" to knock over the bowling pins. When they get all 3 pins down, the caterpillar will have turned into a butterfly! Repeat until all the children have had a turn.

6. COOL-DOWN

Have the children sing the following song to the tune of "Are You Sleeping?"

Caterpillar, caterpillar,
Crawling by, crawling by.
Turn into a butterfly, Turn into a butterfly.
Spread your wings.
Fly away!

7. FINE MOTOR

Give each child a coffee filter and ask them to use markers to draw circles and other shapes on the coffee filter. This will be the butterfly "wings." Next, have the children gather the coffee filter together in the center by pinching it, then clip on a clothespin. Finally, thread a pipe cleaner through the end of the clothespin and twist it into antennae.

Materials

- *The Caterpillow Fight* by Sam McBratney, illustrated by Jill Barton (Candlewick Press/Scholastic, 1996)
- Pillowcases stuffed with several beanbags
- Balance beam
- Streamers – 2 for each child (made from crepe paper, ribbon, scarves, etc.)
- 6 bowling pins (paper towel tubes or commercially purchased plastic pins) with butterfly stickers on each
- 2 balls
- Coffee filters – 1 for each child
- Markers
- Clothespins – 1 for each child
- Pipe cleaners – 1 for each child

* *Here and throughout the lessons, positions designated with an * are described and illustrated in the Appendix on pages 155-157.*

THEME: CIRCUS

LESSON PLAN (QUICK VIEW)

1. **Warm-Up:** Circus action song
2. **Vestibular:** Hula-hoops lion jump
3. **Proprioception:** Elephant walk in styrofoam "peanuts"
4. **Balance:** Tightrope walking (umbrella optional)
5. **Eye-Hand Coordination:** Seal beach ball volley
6. **Cool-Down:** Book: *Henrietta Circus Star* by Sid Hoff
7. **Fine Motor:** Paper plate clown face

1. WARM-UP

Action song "Did You Ever See a Clown?"
Sung to: "Did You Ever See Lassie?"
(From www.preschooleducation.com; original author unknown. Used with permission.)

> Did you ever see a clown, a clown, a clown.
> Did you ever see a clown, move this way and that?
> Move this way and that way, and this way and that way.
> Did you ever see a clown move this way and that?

Have the children sing several times while the teacher leader shows them different ways to move their bodies, such as marching in place, swinging arms up and down, bending knees up and down, etc.

2. VESTIBULAR

Prepare ahead of time by taping crepe paper streamers to several hula-hoops. The hoops will be pretend fire rings for the "lions" to jump through. While an adult holds the hula-hoops in an upright position, the children take turns crawling through the "fire" ring pretending to be a lion. (*Note: Explain to the children that only trained circus lions can jump through a real ring of fire, and that they are never to try this because they might get burned.*)

3. PROPRIOCEPTION

Place styrofoam peanuts inside a wide shallow box. Explain to the children that circus elephants like peanuts, and that they are going to pretend to be stomping elephants walking through peanuts. Have the children form a line and take turns stomping through the box of styrofoam peanuts.

4. BALANCE

Set up several jump ropes on the floor. Explain to the children that at the circus there is often a talented person who can walk and balance on a tightrope. The children can take turns walking on the jump ropes and keeping their balance. (Optional: The children take turns holding an umbrella as a prop.) Play circus music during this activity.

5. EYE-HAND COORDINATION

Have the children pretend to be seals and volley a beach ball around in a circle. They can use their hands, heads, or noses!

6. COOL-DOWN

Read a book about a circus. One example is *Henrietta Circus Star* by Sid Hoff (Garrard Publishing Company, 1978). Discuss all the different events and characters that are associated with a circus, such as clowns, acrobats, trained animals performing tricks, etc.

7. FINE MOTOR

Give each child a paper plate to use for a clown face. Have the children draw facial features on their paper plate. Give them a triangle cut from construction paper for a clown hat. Let the children decorate their clown hats with stickers and cotton balls, and then glue yarn "hair" on the sides of their plates.

Materials

* 2-3 hula-hoops with crepe paper streamers taped on for a "ring of fire"
* Wide shallow box with styrofoam peanuts inside
* Jump ropes
* (Optional: Umbrella prop)
* Circus music
* Beach balls
* *Henrietta Circus Star* by Sid Hoff (Garrard Publishing Company, 1978)
* Paper plates – 1 for each child
* Large construction paper triangle clown hats – 1 for each child
* Stickers, cotton balls, yarn
* Glue, crayons, or markers

THEME: COLORS

LESSON PLAN (QUICK VIEW)

1. **Warm-Up:** Muscle "wake-up" with colorful beanbags
2. **Vestibular:** Obstacle course color path to drop beanbags in a bucket
3. **Proprioception:** Large therapy ball games
4. **Balance:** Color action song by Hap Palmer
5. **Eye-Hand Coordination:** Streamers activities
6. **Cool-Down:** Book: *White Rabbit's Color Book* by Alan Baker
7. **Fine Motor:** Finger painting with different colors

1. WARM-UP

Have the children hold a colorful beanbag and rub it vigorously on each body part for a few seconds, as instructed by the group leader. For example, the leader might say "wake up your head!" or "wake up your arm!," etc. Have the children identify the color of their beanbag.

2. VESTIBULAR

Set up a variety of colorful equipment for the obstacle course. This may include a tunnel in bright red and yellow colors, stepping stones of different colors, and hula-hoops of different colors. Show the students how to move through the obstacle course and have them name the colors as they move on or through each piece of equipment. Repeat several times. Monitor the children's activity level and move onto the next task before they get too excitable. Please refer to Chapter 5 for suggestions on monitoring the group activity level.

3. PROPRIOCEPTION

Use large therapy balls of any color and have the children tall kneel* in a circle to push the ball around the circle using both hands. Have the children lie in supine flexion position* and kick the ball around the circle with both feet. Finally, have the children lie on their stomach while the teacher rolls the ball on their backs for deep-pressure touch for calming.

4. BALANCE

Have each child hold a different-colored card (red, blue, yellow, green) while listening to Hap Palmer's "Colors" action song. Ask them to identify the color of card they are holding, and then begin the activity.

5. EYE-HAND COORDINATION

Give each child a colored crepe paper streamer and have them imitate the leader. The leader pretends to draw in the air with the colored streamer. For example, the leader may paint a fence (move the steamer up/down), paint a house (move a streamer back/forth), draw a circle, square, or plus sign, wave a flag above their heads, or plant some grass (wiggle the streamer down on the ground). This will help the children learn directional concepts, prepositions, and pre-writing skills.

6. COOL-DOWN

Read a book. *White Rabbit's Color Book* by Alan Baker is one example (Houghton Mifflin Company, 1999). Teach the children about mixing 2 colors together to make a new color.

7. FINE MOTOR

Provide finger paint in primary colors for each child with some finger paint paper. Demonstrate how they can mix the colors to create new colors. For children with tactile defensiveness, prepare their hands by firmly rubbing a soft-bristle baby hairbrush across their palms prior to painting.

Materials

- Different-colored beanbags – 1 for each child
- Items for obstacle course (e.g., tunnel, stepping stones, hula-hoops, balance beam)
- 1-3 large therapy balls
- Colored cards (may be laminated) – 1 for each child (blue, yellow, red, green)
- Hap Palmer *Learning Basic Skills Through Music,* "Colors" song (Educational Activities Inc., 1994)
- Crepe paper streamers (different colors)
- *White Rabbit's Color Book* by Alan Baker (Houghton Mifflin Company, 1999)
- Finger paint and paper (red, blue, yellow)

THEME: COWBOYS

LESSON PLAN (QUICK VIEW)

1. **Warm-Up:** Book: *Just Like My Dad* by Tricia Gardella
2. **Vestibular:** Hobby horse relay
3. **Proprioception:** Lasso tug-of-war
4. **Balance:** Barrel "horse" ride
5. **Eye-Hand Coordination:** Lasso ring toss
6. **Cool-Down:** Bandanna dance
7. **Fine Motor:** Cowboy boot collage

1. WARM-UP

Read a book about cowboys. One example is *Just Like My Dad* by Tricia Gardella illustrated by Argot Apple (Caroline House Boyds Mills Press, 1993). If choosing another book, be sure to read one that includes information about lassos, horses, and cowboy clothes so the children can learn vocabulary and concepts related to the theme.

2. VESTIBULAR

Have 3-4 hobby horses for the children to take turns riding by galloping around a path. Play country and western music in the background.

3. PROPRIOCEPTION

Stretch a thick, long rope across the room. Divide the children into two groups and play tug-of-war. Reinforce the concept of a cowboy pulling a lasso.

4. BALANCE

Place a large barrel on its side and have 2-3 children take turns straddling the barrel while rocking it gently back and forth. (Optional: Have the children wear cowboy hats and say "giddy-up, horse!")

5. EYE-HAND COORDINATION

Divide the children into 2-3 groups. For each group, an adult holds up a hobby horse while the children stand about 3 feet from the horse and toss 3 rings around its neck. Repeat several times. The rings can be made of plastic tubing wrapped with electrical tape to keep its shape.

6. COOL-DOWN

Give each child a Bandanna. Sing the following song while waving the Bandanna in the air.
Sung to: "Are You Sleeping?"
(From www.preschooleducation.com; used with permission.)

> Let's go riding, let's go riding,
> Saddle up. Saddle up.
> Everybody ready? Everybody ready?
> Giddyap! Giddyap!

In addition, the children can sing the action song.
Sung to: "I'm a Little Teapot"

> I'm a little cowboy. Here is my hat. (*Point to self, then to top of head*)
> Here are my spurs. (*Point to your heels*)
> And here are my chaps. (*Pat legs*)
> As soon as I wake up (*Stretch, pretend to wake up*)
> I work all day. (*Pretend to lasso a cow*)
> I get on my horse and ride away. (*Pretend to gallop on a horse*)

7. FINE MOTOR

Enlarge the picture of the cowboy boot on page 160. Make copies on construction paper – 4 for each child. Cut small pieces of tactile material (sandpaper, cloth, felt, etc.) and allow the children to glue them onto the cowboy boot. Squeeze glue into a milk lid and use a Q-tip to spread the glue.

Materials

- *Just Like My Dad* by Tricia Gardella (Caroline House Boyds Mills Press, 1993)
- 3-5 hobby horses
- Country/western music
- Long, thick rope
- Large barrel (cowboy hats optional)
- Rings – 3 for each hobby horse. These may be made by forming a ring with plastic tubing and securing with colored electrical tape.
- Bandannas – 1 for each child
- Picture of the outline of a cowboy boot on page 160. Copy one for each child on construction paper
- Tactile materials (small pieces) such as felt, cloth, sandpaper
- Glue, Q-tips, milk container lids

THEME: DENTAL HEALTH

LESSON PLAN (QUICK VIEW)

1. **Warm-Up:** Song: "If you're Happy and You Know It"
2. **Vestibular:** Tooth-to-tooth jumping game
3. **Proprioception:** Theraband dental floss
4. **Balance:** "Toothbrush" balance beam game
5. **Eye-Hand Coordination:** Plastic food throw in box "mouth"
6. **Cool-Down:** Book: *Going to the Dentist* by Mercer Mayer
7. **Fine Motor:** White paper teeth snip-and-glue

1. WARM-UP

Have the children sing the familiar song "If You're Happy and You Know It."

If you're happy and you know it, show your teeth,
If you're happy and you know it, show your teeth,
If you're happy and you know it, then your face will really show it,
If you're happy and you know it, show your teeth!"

Repeat with: . . . brush your teeth; floss your teeth; shout hurray; smile real big.

2. VESTIBULAR

Tape large construction paper teeth to the floor in a circle pattern. Have the children jump from tooth to tooth around the circle. They may also perform other locomotor actions such as bear walking,* galloping,* sliding, etc. Have them work on pre-math skills by counting the number of teeth on the floor.

3. PROPRIOCEPTION

Teach the children about the importance of flossing teeth and show them real dental floss. Give each child a 2-foot piece of theraband. Have them hold the theraband with both hands, place it under one foot, and pull by alternating arms up/down to imitate flossing. Have them place the theraband under the other foot and repeat.

4. BALANCE

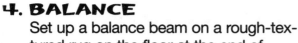

Set up a balance beam on a rough-textured rug on the floor at the end of the beam. Explain to the children that the balance beam is a pretend toothbrush handle and the rug is the brush. The children may take their shoes off for this activity. Have the children stand in a line, walk across the balance beam, and step onto the rug. Repeat several times.

5. EYE-HAND COORDINATION

Prepare ahead of time a large box "mouth" by cutting a hole in a box and drawing a face on it with teeth around the hole. Teach the children about how nutritious food can keep teeth healthy. The children take turns throwing 3 pieces of plastic pretend food into the "mouth."

6. COOL-DOWN

Read a book about teeth or dentists. One example is *Going to the Dentist* by Mercer Mayer (Golden Books Publishing Company, 1990). Discuss healthy habits for good dental health.

7. FINE MOTOR

The children snip small "teeth" from white strips of paper. Have them glue the "teeth" to a picture of the reproducible mouth on page 161.

Materials
- Large white construction paper teeth (10-12) and tape
- A 2-foot piece of theraband for each child
- Balance beam
- Textured rug
- Large box with a hole cut in it and a face drawn on the outside
- Plastic play food, spot marker
- *Going to the Dentist* by Mercer Mayer (Golden Books Publishing Company, 1990)
- 2-3 white paper strips about 1x8" long
- Scissors, glue
- Picture of the mouth on page 161 – 1 for each child
- Dental floss

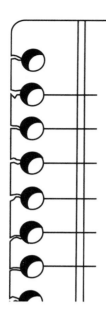

THEME: DINOSAURS

LESSON PLAN (QUICK VIEW)

1. **Warm-Up:** Dinosaur movement chant
2. **Vestibular:** Dinosaur footprints obstacle course
3. **Proprioception:** Dinosaur heavy block "bones"
4. **Balance:** Dinosaur "Hokey Pokey"
5. **Eye-Hand Coordination:** Dinosaur egg pass
6. **Cool-Down:** Book: *How Do Dinosaurs Say Goodnight?* by Jane Yolen
7. **Fine Motor:** Textured dinosaur

1. WARM-UP

Sung to: "Teddy Bear, Teddy Bear"

Dinosaur, dinosaur, turn around.
Dinosaur, dinosaur, stomp on the ground.
Dinosaur, dinosaur, give a roar.
Dinosaur, dinosaur, jump off the floor.
Dinosaur, dinosaur, swing your tail.
Dinosaur, dinosaur, "Whew, you smell!"
(*Plug nose with fingers*)

2. VESTIBULAR

Set up an obstacle course using a tunnel, balance beam, and paper dinosaur footprints. Have the children move through the obstacle course pretending to be dinosaurs. Have the children crawl through the tunnel (cave), walk across the balance beam (fallen tree trunk), and stomp/jump on the dinosaur footprints. Repeat several times.

3. PROPRIOCEPTION

Divide the children into 2 groups. Put blocks inside a small box (pretend dinosaur bones), and have the children carry them across the room and back again, being careful not to drop the bones! Have one child from each group go at the same time. It is helpful to place a turn-around marker at the other end of the room.

4. BALANCE

"Dino-Pokey"
Sung to: "Hokey Pokey"
(*From www.preschooleducation.com; used with permission.*)

You put your claws in
You put your claws out

You put your claws in
scratch 'em all about
You do the Dino-Pokey and you turn yourself about.
That's what it's all about.

Additional Verse:
Feet in/feet out/stomp them all about
Teeth in/teeth out/chomp them all about
Tail in/tail out/wag it all about

5. EYE-HAND COORDINATION

Have the children sit in a circle. Fill plastic Easter eggs with sand or rice and tape them closed. Tell the children that these are dinosaur eggs and that they must be very careful not to drop them. Play music in the background while the children pass the eggs around the circle. Stop the music and have the children pass the eggs in the opposite direction. Repeat several times.

6. COOL-DOWN

Read a book about dinosaurs. One example is *How Do Dinosaurs Say Goodnight?* by Jane Yolen (Scholastic, Inc., 2000).

7. FINE MOTOR

Give the children each a copy of the dinosaur picture on page 162. Using Q-tips dipped in glue, have the children glue a variety of textures onto the dinosaur picture. This may include cereal, small pieces of sandpaper, cotton balls, aluminum foil, wallpaper samples, tissue paper, fabric, etc.

Materials

- Tunnel
- Balance beam
- Paper dinosaur footprints
- 2 small boxes with blocks
- Several plastic Easter eggs with sand or rice inside (taped closed)
- Music
- *How Do Dinosaurs Say Goodnight?* by Jane Yolen (Scholastic, Inc. 2000)
- Outline picture of a dinosaur on page 162 – 1 for each child
- Textured materials (e.g., cereal, small pieces of sandpaper, cotton balls, aluminum foil, wallpaper samples, tissue paper, fabric)
- Glue and Q-tips

THEME: DOCTOR

LESSON PLAN (QUICK VIEW)

1. **Warm-Up:** Magic lotion potion
2. **Vestibular:** Monkeys jumping on the bed
3. **Proprioception:** Scooter board ambulance
4. **Balance:** Balance beam/pick up doctor supplies
5. **Eye-Hand Coordination:** Toss/catch rolled Ace bandage
6. **Cool-Down:** Book: *My Doctor* by Harlow Rockwell
7. **Fine Motor:** Construction paper doctor's bag

1. WARM-UP

Tell the children that the lotion is a magical potion, and that if they rub it on their muscles, they will get stronger. While the children are sitting in a circle, give each of them a squirt of lotion in the palms of their hands and have them rub it on their arms, hands, elbow, legs, knees, ankles, etc., labeling the body parts as they go.

2. VESTIBULAR

Place a large mat in the center of the circle of children. Have 5 children stand on the mat. The other children can help say the monkey action poem while the 5 children on the mat jump up and down.

> Five little monkeys jumping on the bed. (*Show five fingers*)
> One fell off and bumped his head. (*Touch hand to head*)
> Mama called the doctor and the doctor said, (*Pretend hand phone to ear*)
> "No more monkeys jumping on the bed!" (*Shake index finger*)

Repeat several times. Do not have a child actually fall down; simply have the child continue to jump as the children repeat the monkey action song a few times. Then have 5 more children stand on the mat and take a turn jumping while the other children sing the monkey song.
(*Note: An exercise mini-trampoline may be used alongside the mat with one child at a time taking a turn. Be sure to have an adult standing near for safety.*)

3. PROPRIOCEPTION

Use 2 scooter boards as pretend ambulances. Have one child sit on a scooter board and hold a doll, while another child pushes the "ambulance" to the "hospital" (a designated location across the room) and back across the floor to the starting point. Have the children switch places. Repeat until all the children have had a turn to both push and ride the scooter board ambulance.

4. BALANCE

Set up a balance beam. Place toy pretend plastic doctor's supplies on the floor alongside the balance beam. (Examples include stethoscopes, tongue depressors, cotton balls, Q-tips, bandages, medicine bottles, etc.). Have the children walk across the balance beam, one at a time, each picking up one item from the floor while trying to stay on the balance beam.

5. EYE-HAND COORDINATION

Have the children toss and catch rolled-up Ace bandages either to a partner or around a circle of children.

6. COOL-DOWN

Read a book about doctors. One example is *My Doctor* by Harlow Rockwell (Macmillan Press, 1973). Discuss why we need to visit a doctor when we are sick, so that we can get well, etc.

7. FINE MOTOR

Give each child an 11x14" piece of black or white construction paper. Have them fold it in half and round the corners using scissors. Then ask them to draw a symbol of a red cross on the outside of the folded paper with chalk. Next, they glue or tape a variety of medical supplies onto the inside of the construction paper doctor's bag, such as a tongue depressor, Q-tip, cotton ball, gauze, and a peel-and-stick a bandage. Finally, punch holes at the opening of the bag and thread a pipe cleaner through it to create a handle to carry the doctor's bag.

Materials

- Lotion (use hypo-allergenic lotion for children with skin sensitivity. Also consider the scent of the lotion; for example, use vanilla or lavender for calming, or citrus for alerting. Use non-scented lotion if any of the children have high sensitivity to smell)
- Large mat
- (Optional: Exercise mini-trampoline)
- 2 scooter boards
- Dolls
- Balance beam
- Doctor's supplies such as stethoscope, medicine bottles, cotton balls, Q-tips, gauze, bandages, tongue depressor (some of these items may also be used for the fine-motor project)
- Several rolled Ace bandages
- *My Doctor* by Harlow Rockwell (Macmillan Press, 1973)
- 11x14" black or white construction paper – 1 for each child
- Chalk, crayon, or markers
- Glue, tape, scissors, hole punch
- Pipe cleaners – 1 for each child
- Q-tips, cotton balls, bandages, tongue depressors, gauze – 1 each for each child

THEME: EARTH DAY/RECYCLE
LESSON PLAN (QUICK VIEW)

1. **Warm-Up:** Action song: "Picking up the Trash and Put It in the Trash Can"
2. **Vestibular:** Relay race to recycle aluminum cans and plastic bottles
3. **Proprioception:** Gallon milk jug crush
4. **Balance:** Pretend plant-a-tree
5. **Eye-Hand Coordination:** Newspaper throw into recycle box
6. **Cool-Down:** Book: *Dear Children of the Earth* by Schim Schimmel
7. **Fine Motor:** Collage with variety of recycle materials

1. WARM-UP

Teach the children the following song and have them practice singing it a couple of times. Sung to: "The Paw Paw Patch"

Picking up the trash and put it in the trash can.
Picking up the trash and put it in the trash can.
Picking up the trash and put it in the trash can, let's clean up our earth!

2. VESTIBULAR

Divide the children into 2 teams. Place 2 boxes side by side at one end of the room. Label the boxes with a recycle symbol (see page 163) and tape a plastic bottle to the front of one box and an aluminum can to the other. Have one child from each team carry an aluminum can or a plastic bottle across the room, put it in the appropriate box, and move back in line for the next child. The children can move in a variety of ways such as hopping, walking backward, galloping, etc. Continue until all the children have had at least 2 turns.

3. PROPRIOCEPTION

Save empty, clean milk jugs and remove the lids (save the lids for fine-motor activity). Give one milk jug to each child and let them push with their feet and hands to smash the milk jugs flat.

4. BALANCE

Explain to the children that trees help the earth and help people to breathe. The more trees we have, the better. Have the children pretend they are trees growing from tiny seeds. They crouch down low into a seed shape and slowly move to stand up. Then they balance on one foot with arms stretched out wide like tree branches.

5. EYE-HAND COORDINATION

Put a box in the center of the circle of children. Give each child a piece of newspaper to crumble. Let them take turns "recycling" the newspaper by tossing it into the box.

6. COOL-DOWN

Read a book about Earth Day or recycling. One example is *Dear Children of the Earth* by Schim Schimmel (Northword Press, Inc., 1994). Explain in simple terms how important recycling is to our earth – for the trees, animals, oceans, streams, and the air we breathe.

7. FINE MOTOR

Give each child a large piece of construction paper and a variety of cut-up recyclable materials to glue on the paper to create a collage. Use Q-tips dipped in glue to increase fine-motor prehension. Examples of suitable materials include sandpaper, cloth, cardboard, felt, plastic bubble wrap, etc.

Materials

- Pieces of paper trash
- Trash can
- 2 boxes with recycle symbol (page 163) taped to the front (one of these boxes may be used for the newspaper toss game)
- Aluminum cans and plastic bottles (1 plastic bottle, 1 aluminum can)
- Empty milk jugs (clean with no lids) – 1 for each child
- Newspaper
- Large sheet of construction paper – 1 for each child
- Variety of recyclable materials cut up into small pieces; examples include sandpaper, cloth, cardboard, felt, plastic bubble wrap, etc.
- Glue poured into milk jug lids
- Q-tips to dip in glue
- *Dear Children of the Earth* by Schim Schimmel (Northword Press, Inc., 1994)

THEME: EGGS

LESSON PLAN (QUICK VIEW)

1. **Warm-Up:** "Egg Hunt" song
2. **Vestibular:** Obstacle course to get eggs
3. **Proprioception:** Smash the kid "egg"
4. **Balance:** Balance beam egg spoon relay
5. **Eye-Hand Coordination:** Plastic egg toss into a basket
6. **Cool-Down:** Book: *The Great Easter Egg Hunt* by Suzy-Jane Tanner
7. **Fine Motor:** Paper plate baskets

1. WARM-UP

Place plastic eggs around the room, 1 for each child. Place a basket in the center of the circle of children. Explain to the children that they are going to hop like a bunny to find a plastic egg, put it in the basket, and then sit back down where they started. Teach them the following song, have them practice singing it, and then begin the activity.

"Egg Hunt" song
Sung to: "Paw Paw Patch"
(From www.preschooleducation.com; original author unknown. Used with permission.)

Hunting for eggs;
Put 'em in my basket.
Hunting for eggs;
Put 'em in my basket.
Hunting for eggs;
Put 'em in my basket.
Now my basket's full.

2. VESTIBULAR

Set up an obstacle course with beanbag chairs to crawl over, chair to crawl under, tunnel to crawl through, paper eggs to jump on, etc. Show the children how to move through the obstacle course. They are going to pretend to go on an egg hunt as they move through the obstacle course. Let them each pick up a plastic egg as they move along the obstacle course and put the egg in a basket when they get to the end. Repeat several times.

3. PROPRIOCEPTION

Tell the children they are going to pretend to be an egg hatching into a baby chick. Have the children curl up into an "egg" shape. Gently "smash" the kid eggs by placing a beanbag on top of them. (Do not cover their head.) After the children are finished being "smashed," they pretend to be a baby chick hatching out of the egg by pushing the beanbag chair off their body and standing up. They can even make chirping sounds! Repeat until all the children have had a turn to be smashed and all are calm and relaxed. (*Note: If you have more than one beanbag chair, several children can take turns simultaneously.*)

4. BALANCE
Set up a balance beam and have the children form a line at one end. Give each child a spoon with a plastic egg on it. Have the children attempt to walk across the balance beam carrying the egg on the spoon without dropping it. For children who have extreme difficulty with this activity, use a taped line on the floor to walk on.

5. EYE-HAND COORDINATION
Divide the children into 2 teams. Place a basket about 5 feet from a place marker – 1 for each team. Have each "team" take turns standing on their place marker and tossing 3 plastic eggs into their basket.

6. COOL-DOWN
Read a book about eggs. One example is *The Great Easter Egg Hunt* by Suzy-Jane Tanner (HarperCollins, 1996). You can also choose a general book about eggs or chickens.

7. FINE MOTOR
Give each child a large paper plate. Have them draw circle "eggs" on the center of the plate and color it using different-colored crayons. Using a paper punch, punch 2 holes in the paper plate on opposite sides. Have the children lace a pipe cleaner through the holes and pull it tight so that the paper plate curls upward into a "basket" shape. Let the children glue plastic grass in the center of the paper plate.

Materials
- Plastic eggs – at least 1 for each child
- 2 baskets
- Obstacle course equipment – chair, tunnel, paper eggs taped to floor
- Beanbag chair(s)
- Balance beam (tape line optional)
- Spoons – 1 for each child
- 2 place markers
- *The Great Easter Egg Hunt* by Suzy-Jane Tanner (HarperCollins, 1996)
- Large paper plates – 1 for each child
- Crayons, glue, paper punch
- Plastic grass
- Pipe cleaners

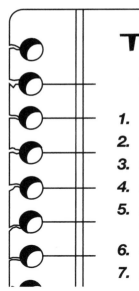

THEME: EVERGREEN TREE

LESSON PLAN (QUICK VIEW)

1. **Warm-Up:** Song: "I'm a Little Pine Tree"
2. **Vestibular:** Musical chairs – matching tree ornaments
3. **Proprioception:** Chop down and carry tree
4. **Balance:** "Kid" tree decorations
5. **Eye-Hand Coordination:** Marshmallow throw through a wreath
6. **Cool-Down:** Book: *The Snow Tree* by Caroline Repchuk
7. **Fine Motor:** Snip, snip, pine tree

1. WARM-UP

"I'm a Little Pine Tree"
Sung to: "I'm A Little Teapot"
(From www.preschooleducation.com; original author unknown. Used with permission.)

> I'm a little pine tree – as you can see,
> All the other pine trees are bigger than me.
> Maybe when I grow up – then I'll be
> A great big merry holiday tree!

2. VESTIBULAR

Play a game of musical chairs. Place chairs in a line back to back – 1 for each child. Tape a simple picture, to represent an ornament, on each chair. Give a matching picture ornament to each child. Play holiday music. While the music is playing, have the children move in a circle around the line of chairs. Tell the children that when the music stops, they are to find the chair with the matching ornament and sit on that chair. Repeat. Have the children move in different ways each time, such as bear walking,* galloping,* tiptoeing, etc.

3. PROPRIOCEPTION

Explain to the children that they are going to pretend to find a pine tree at a farm, cut the tree down, and bring it "home." Place a large-sized bolster upright. Have 3-4 students work together to pretend they are chopping down the tree by pushing it. Then have them work together to pick up the bolster "tree" and carry it across the room to their "home." Repeat until all the students have had a turn. If a bolster is not available, a cardboard tube from a carpet roll may be used or a small rug rolled up.

4. BALANCE

Have the children pretend to decorate a "kid" evergreen tree. Divide the students into groups of 2-3. One child pretends to be the tree and stands with arms stretched out wide, while the other child decorates. Use paper ornaments with strings attached and pipe cleaner ornaments to hang on the "tree" child's fingers, ears, arms, etc. Strands of garland may also be gently draped over the "tree" child's shoulders and outstretched arms. The "tree" child will attempt to balance on one foot after the decorations are complete. Be sure all the children have a turn to be the "tree."

5. EYE-HAND COORDINATION

Wrap 9 marshmallows in plastic wrap (red/green holiday plastic wrap, if available). Divide the children into 3 groups and have them stand in a line behind a place marker. Have an adult stand by each place marker about 5 feet away holding up a wreath. The children take turns with 3 attempts each to throw marshmallows through the wreath.

6. COOL-DOWN

Read a book about evergreen trees. *The Snow Tree* by Caroline Repchuk, illustrated by Josephine Martin, is one example (The Templar Company, 1996). Felt props may be made to accompany the book as a flannel board story. In the discussion, name and describe the animals who bring decorations for the tree, and what color each decoration is.

7. FINE MOTOR

Cut circles out of green construction paper (about 5 inches in diameter), 1 for each child. Draw a line from the peripheral to the center using a thick black marker. Have the children snip all around the circle and cut the line. An adult curls the paper into a cone tree shape and staples it. Next, the children curl up the fringes on the edge, drip glue from a bottle around the tree, and sprinkle glitter on the glue by pinching the glitter with index finger and thumb. Finally, have the children place a sticker star on the top.

Materials

- Pair of matching paper picture ornaments (may be made from die cuts) – 1 set for each child
- Holiday music
- Large-sized bolster, or cardboard tube from carpet roll, or rolled-up rug
- Tree decorations: garlands, pipe cleaner ornaments, paper ornaments with strings attached for hanging
- 9 marshmallows in plastic wrap (Optional: Use red/green holiday plastic wrap)
- 3 wreaths
- 3 place markers
- *The Snow Tree* by Caroline Repchuk (The Templar Company, 1996)
- (Optional: Felt props for flannel board story to accompany *The Snow Tree*)
- Green construction paper circles (about 5 inches in diameter) – 1 for each child
- Scissors, glue, glitter, star sticker, stapler

THEME: FALL LEAVES

LESSON PLAN (QUICK VIEW)

1. **Warm-Up:** Song: "The Leaves on the Trees"
2. **Vestibular:** Log roll on top of leaves on a mat
3. **Proprioception:** Beanbag "leaf pile" jump
4. **Balance:** Balance beam holding streamer leaves
5. **Eye-Hand Coordination:** beanbag toss into a leaf "bag" bucket
6. **Cool-Down:** Book: *Fall Leaves* by Mary Packard
7. **Fine Motor:** Tactile leaf picture

1. WARM-UP

"The Leaves on the Trees"
Sung to: "The Wheels on the Bus"
(From www.preschooleducation.com; original author unknown. Used with permission.)

Give each child 1 red and 1 orange laminated paper leaf (copy reproducible leaf on page 164.) Sing the following verse while the children hold up the correct leaf color:
"The leaves on the trees turn orange and red, orange and red, orange and red, the leaves on the trees turn orange and red, all around the town."

Next, the children stand up and sing the following verse while making the leaves tumble to the floor:
"The leaves on the tree come tumbling down, tumbling down, tumbling down, the leaves on the tree come tumbling down, all around the town."

For this verse, the children "swish" their leaves across the floor:
"The leaves on the trees go swish, swish, swish … swish, swish, swish … swish, swish, swish … the leaves on the trees go swish, swish, swish, all around the town."

For the last verse, have the children place their leaves on the floor in front of them:
"We'll rake them in a pile and jump right in, jump right in, jump right in … we'll rake them in a pile and jump right in all around the town."

2. VESTIBULAR

Place a mat in the middle of the room and have the children sit around the outside of it. Place a few dried leaves across the surface of the mat and have the children take turns log rolling* down the mat and back again. Listen to the leaves crunch.

3. PROPRIOCEPTION

Set up 2-3 large beanbag chairs. Divide the children into small groups. Taking one turn at a time, have each child jump into the beanbag chair landing on their knees, then lie on their tummy. Gently press on the child's back with open-palm hands to give firm-pressure touch while they are in the beanbag chair.

4. BALANCE

Give each child orange and red leaves from the warm-up song. Have them walk across the balance beam while waving the leaves. Repeat for several minutes. Music may be playing in the background.

5. EYE-HAND COORDINATION

Set up 2-3 buckets that are partially filled with leaves. Divide the children into small groups and allow each child to take a turn tossing a beanbag into the bucket. Give them 3 beanbags per turn. The child should be standing about 5 feet from the bucket. It is helpful to have the children stand on a place marker such as a paper leaf taped to the floor.

6. COOL-DOWN

Read a book about fall. *Fall Leaves* by Mary Packard (Scholastic, 1999) is one example. Discuss the different types of leaves and the reason the leaves fall off trees to prepare for winter.

7. FINE MOTOR

Give the children several dried leaves and have them squeeze the leaves, crunching them into small pieces. Next, have the children spread glue onto a piece of red or orange construction paper inside the outline of the reproducible leaf pattern on page 164. Then they sprinkle the dried leaves on top.

Materials

- Pre-cut or die-cut construction-paper orange and red leaves – 2 per child of each color; see page 164
- Dried leaves (2 buckets full)
- 2-3 beanbag chairs
- Balance beam
- 2 buckets partially filled with dried leaves
- Beanbags (at least 6-9)
- *Fall Leaves* by Mary Packard (Scholastic, 1999)
- Choice of red/orange construction paper with a leaf pattern (page 164)
- Glue squeezed onto a plastic lid
- (Optional: Background music)

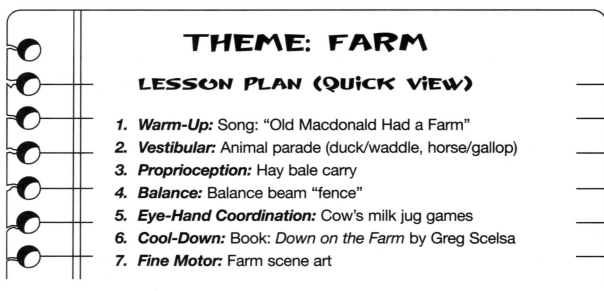

THEME: FARM

LESSON PLAN (QUICK VIEW)

1. **Warm-Up:** Song: "Old Macdonald Had a Farm"
2. **Vestibular:** Animal parade (duck/waddle, horse/gallop)
3. **Proprioception:** Hay bale carry
4. **Balance:** Balance beam "fence"
5. **Eye-Hand Coordination:** Cow's milk jug games
6. **Cool-Down:** Book: *Down on the Farm* by Greg Scelsa
7. **Fine Motor:** Farm scene art

1. WARM-UP
Sing the traditional song "Old Macdonald Had a Farm." Repeat with animal sounds of ducks, horses, cows, pigs, etc.

2. VESTIBULAR
Have the children imitate a variety of animal movements such as waddling like a duck,* galloping* like a horse, or crawling on hands and knees to imitate a cow. The children can make the animal sound while they move.

3. PROPRIOCEPTION
Fill 1-2 boxes with heavy material such as blocks, magazines, etc., and tape them closed. These will be used for pretend hay bales. Have the children stand in a circle and pass the hay bales around. Play music in the background. When the music stops, the children "freeze." When the music starts again, they pass the hay bales around the circle in the opposite direction.

4. BALANCE
Set up a balance beam and have the children pretend it is a fence. Explain that farmers use fences to keep their animals from running away. Show a picture of a fence, so that the children can relate an image to the word. Have them walk on the "fence" and try not to fall off! Repeat several times.

5. EYE-HAND COORDINATION

Prepare ahead of time the following materials: Save several 1-gallon milk jugs. Rinse them clean and cut off the bottom half. (Recycle the bottom half of the milk jugs and save the lids to use as a glue container for the fine-motor activity.) For the activity, discuss where milk comes from and then explain how to play the game. Divide the children into partners or small groups. It works best to have them face each other in a row. Have one child hold the milk jug by the handle. Another child rolls a tennis ball and the partner attempts to "catch" the ball under the milk jug. *(Note: The ball may represent a mouse.)* After a few minutes, have the children switch roles, so that every child gets a chance to use the milk jug.

6. COOL-DOWN

Read a book about farms. *Down on the Farm* by Greg Scelsa (Creative Teaching Press, 1995) is one example. Discuss the different animals that live on a farm. Also talk about farmers, tractors, and crops that are grown on a farm.

7. FINE MOTOR

Give each child a large piece of blue construction paper. Have them create a farm scene by gluing a red square and triangle on the paper to make a "barn," a rectangular piece of aluminum foil for a grain silo, cotton ball for clouds, and crumbled Shredded Wheat cereal for a hay stack.

Materials
- 1-2 small boxes filled with heavy material (magazines, blocks) taped closed
- Music tape/CD (country western)
- Balance beam
- Several clean 1-gallon milk jugs with the bottoms cut off (save the lids)
- Tennis balls
- *Down on the Farm* by Greg Scelsa (Creative Teaching Press, 1995)
- Large piece of blue construction paper – 1 for each child
- Cotton balls
- Shredded Wheat cereal
- Pre-cut red construction paper square and triangle – 1 for each child
- Pre-cut rectangular-shaped aluminum foil – 1 for each child
- Glue put in milk jug lids
- Q-tips to dip in the glue

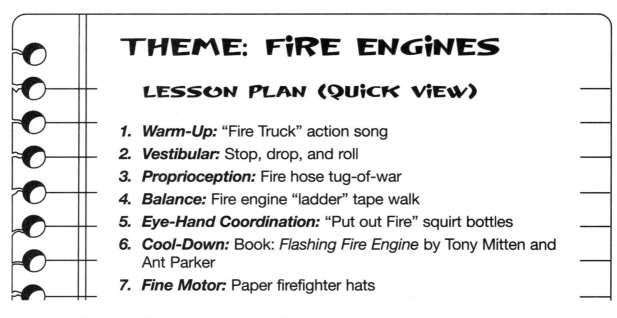

THEME: FIRE ENGINES

LESSON PLAN (QUICK VIEW)

1. **Warm-Up:** "Fire Truck" action song
2. **Vestibular:** Stop, drop, and roll
3. **Proprioception:** Fire hose tug-of-war
4. **Balance:** Fire engine "ladder" tape walk
5. **Eye-Hand Coordination:** "Put out Fire" squirt bottles
6. **Cool-Down:** Book: *Flashing Fire Engine* by Tony Mitten and Ant Parker
7. **Fine Motor:** Paper firefighter hats

1. WARM-UP

Have the children sing the following song and perform the associated actions while seated.

Sung to: "Paw Paw Patch"

Hurry, hurry drive the fire truck. (*Pretend to turn a steering wheel*)
Hurry, hurry drive the fire truck.
Hurry, hurry drive the fire truck.
Ding, ding, ding, ding, ding.

Verse #2: Hurry, hurry climb the ladder …
(*Pretend to climb a ladder using arms only*)

Verse #3: Hurry, hurry, squirt the hoses …
(*Pretend to hold a hose and point it in different directions*)

Verse #4: Hurry, hurry, put out the fire … (*Bang hands on the floor*)

2. VESTIBULAR

Teach the children about fire safety and show them how to avoid smoke by following the "stop, drop, and roll" sequence. Place a mat on the floor and have the children take turns practicing. Repeat at least twice. Be sure the children roll in one direction the first turn and the other direction the second turn.

3. PROPRIOCEPTION

Tell the children that they are going to pretend to be firefighters and that they will use the rope as a hose playing tug-of-war. To prepare for this activity, extend a long rope across the floor and tie a piece of material to represent the center. Next, divide the children into 2 groups. Have 1 group of children hold the rope on one side and the other group hold the rope on the other side. The 2 groups will face each other. (Optional:

Pretend plastic fire hats may be worn as props.) When the teacher announces, "Go," each group of children pulls the rope in opposite directions holding for 20-30 seconds. Have them rest and then repeat for several more times.

4. BALANCE

Create a "ladder" on the floor by using masking tape. (*Note: Best if prepared ahead of time.*) Children take turns, with several walking at the same time on the tape around the ladder attempting to keep their balance. Music may be playing in the background.

5. EYE-HAND COORDINATION

Tape down several paper pictures of fire on the bottom of an empty water table. Using dishwashing soap bottles filled with water, have the children stand around the table squirting water onto the "fire." Tell them to try to put the fire out.

6. COOL-DOWN

Read a book about fire engines or fire safety. One example is *Flashing Fire Engine* by Tony Mitten and Ant Parker (Scholastic, 1988). Discuss the fire safety rules of stop, drop, and roll. Review the exit plan for fire drills in the building.

7. FINE MOTOR

Using the reproducible outline of a firefighter hat on page 165, make one copy for each child with red construction paper. If copies are made with regular white paper, the children can color them red. (You may want to cut them out ahead of time.) Have the children snip pieces of aluminum foil and glue to the fire "hat," then peel and stick a "Jr. Firefighter" sticker onto the front of the "hat." (*Note: These stickers can be obtained from your local fire department.*) Remember to have the children practice writing their "name" (circle, plus, square shapes) on the back of the hat. Finally, staple red construction paper strips on to form a band so the hat can fit around the child's head.

Materials
- Mat
- Long rope
- (Optional: Plastic firefighter hats for props)
- Masking tape used to create a "ladder" pattern on the floor (prepare ahead of time)
- Music CD/tape to play during balance task
- Empty water table with several pictures of fire taped to the bottom
- Dishwashing soap bottles filled with water (squirt bottles may also be used)
- *Flashing Fire Engine* by Tony Mitten and Ant Parker (Scholastic, 1988)
- Copies of firefighter hat outline page 165 on red construction paper or on white with children coloring red (cut out ahead of time)
- Aluminum foil
- Scissors, glue, crayons/pencils, stapler
- "Jr. Firefighter" stickers obtained from your local fire department

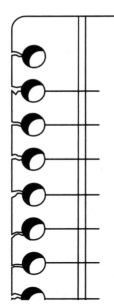

THEME: FRIENDSHIP/ COOPERATION

LESSON PLAN (QUICK VIEW)

1. **Warm-Up:** Friendship cooperation song
2. **Vestibular:** Partner row boats and jumping
3. **Proprioception:** Friends carrying heavy object
4. **Balance:** "Friend to Friend" game
5. **Eye-Hand Coordination:** Balloon volley
6. **Cool-Down:** Book: *Differences* by Gerard Arantowicz
7. **Fine Motor:** Friendship paper chain

1. WARM-UP

Sing the following familiar song "The More We Get Together . . ." while the children pass a heart shape around in a circle. The heart represents cooperation, friendship, and "equality."

> The more we get together, together, together,
> The more we get together, the happier we'll be.
> For your friends are my friends and my friends are your friends.
> The more we get together the happier we'll be.

2. VESTIBULAR

Pair the children with a partner. Have them sit facing each other with legs straight and feet touching and holding hands. Then have them cooperatively rock back and forth. After they have performed this action for a few minutes, have them stand up facing each other and hold hands while jumping up and down cooperatively.

3. PROPRIOCEPTION

With children staying in pairs, use a large therapy ball or another heavy object and have partners/ friends help each other carry it across the room and back again. They can also roll it together while in tall kneeling position.* Have 2-3 pairs take turns simultaneously.

4. BALANCE

Have the children stay with their partners. Call out body parts for the friends to connect. For example, "Back to back, hand to hand, foot to foot, knee to knee, elbow to elbow, etc."

5. EYE-HAND COORDINATION

To prepare for this activity, blow up 2 balloons and draw pictures of people on them. Divide the children into 2 small groups. Have each group stand in a circle and cooperatively volley the balloon around. Try to keep it in the air.

6. COOL-DOWN

Read a book about diversity and cooperation. One example is *Differences* written and illustrated by Gerard Arantowicz (Leathers Publishing, 2002). Explain how people are different, such as different skin color, hair and eye color, wear glasses to help see, use wheelchairs or crutches to help walk, wear hearing aids to help hear, and yet are all the same inside.

7. FINE MOTOR

Have the children cut paper strips about 1" wide from brown, tan, black, and white construction paper. These colors represent different skin colors. The children draw a smiley face on each of the paper strips and create a paper chain. Have children use glue to connect the strip and form a circle, then loop another strip through the circle and glue it closed. Continue until all the strips are glued together. Finally, glue all of the children's chains together to form one long chain and hang it on a bulletin board.

Materials

- Heart shape (paper or plush)
- 2-3 large therapy balls or other heavy object
- 2 balloons with pictures of people drawn on them
- *Differences* written and illustrated by Gerard Arantowicz (Leathers Publishing, 2002)
- Brown, tan, black, white construction paper with lines drawn 1 inch apart
- Scissors, glue, markers

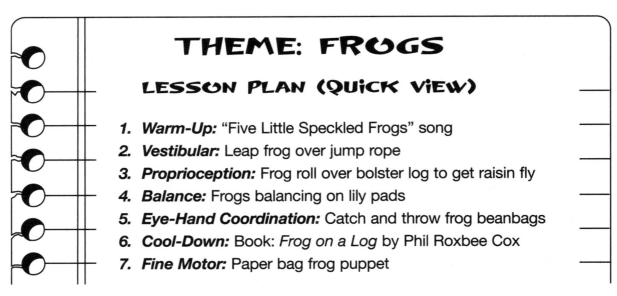

THEME: FROGS
LESSON PLAN (QUICK VIEW)

1. **Warm-Up:** "Five Little Speckled Frogs" song
2. **Vestibular:** Leap frog over jump rope
3. **Proprioception:** Frog roll over bolster log to get raisin fly
4. **Balance:** Frogs balancing on lily pads
5. **Eye-Hand Coordination:** Catch and throw frog beanbags
6. **Cool-Down:** Book: *Frog on a Log* by Phil Roxbee Cox
7. **Fine Motor:** Paper bag frog puppet

1. WARM-UP
"Five Little Speckled Frogs"

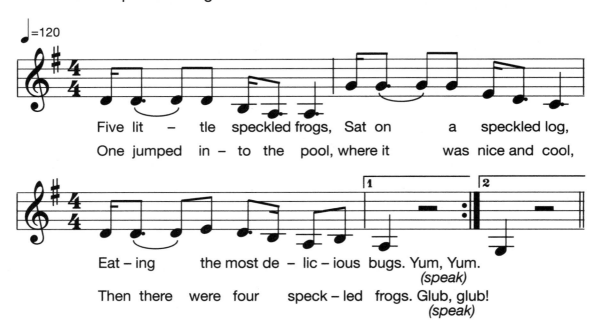

Five lit – tle speckled frogs, Sat on a speckled log,
One jumped in – to the pool, where it was nice and cool,

Eat – ing the most de – lic – ious bugs. Yum, Yum. *(speak)*
Then there were four speck – led frogs. Glub, glub! *(speak)*

Repeat for 4 frogs, 3 frogs, 2 frogs and 1 frog.
Have children squat on the floor like frogs.* One by one, the children take turns to be the frog that jumps into the pool.

2. VESTIBULAR
Place a jump rope across the floor. Have the children form a line in front of the rope. Demonstrate squatting and hopping like a frog.* Have the children take turns hopping like a frog over the jump rope. Repeat several times.

3. PROPRIOCEPTION

Allow each child to take turns pretending to be a frog on a log and eating a fly. One child at a time rolls over a large bolster (pretend log) on their tummy using their arms to support their trunk. They then attempt to get a raisin (pretend fly) off the floor using only their tongue. (*Note: Place each raisin on a separate paper towel between children for sanitation.*)

4. BALANCE

Cut green construction paper lily pads and tape them to the floor. Have the children imitate the teacher leader performing a variety of balance tasks using the lily pads. For example, the children can stand on one foot, hop on one foot, hop around the lily pads, side to side or over the "lily pads."

5. EYE-HAND COORDINATION

Divide the children into partners. Give each pair of children a beanbag frog. Have them toss and catch the frog back and forth to each other.

6. COOL-DOWN

Read a book about frogs. One example is *Frog on a Log* by Phil Roxbee Cox, illustrated by Stephen Cartwright (Usborne Publishing, 2001). Discuss what types of bugs frogs like to eat, where they live, how they like to move by hopping, and what sound they make. The children can imitate the sound of a frog, "ribbit, ribbit."

7. FINE MOTOR

Have the children color and cut out the frog pattern on page 166. Then have them glue it to a paper bag. Remember to have them practice writing their "names" on the paper sack ("name" = circle, plus, square).

Materials
- Jump rope
- Large bolster
- Raisins, paper towels
- Green construction paper lily pads
- Beanbag frogs
- *Frog on a Log* by Phil Roxbee Cox, illustrated by Stephen Cartwright (Usborne Publishing, 2001)
- Reproducible frog pattern on page 166
- Paper bags – 1 for each child
- Small pieces of green crayons, scissors, glue

THEME: GROUNDHOG DAY

LESSON PLAN (QUICK VIEW)

1. **Warm-Up:** Book: *Groundhog Day* by Betsy Lewin
2. **Vestibular:** Groundhog jump out of box
3. **Proprioception:** Groundhog cloth tunnel
4. **Balance:** Shadow partners
5. **Eye-Hand Coordination:** Flashlight shadows
6. **Cool-Down:** Shadow song
7. **Fine Motor:** Paper cup groundhog pop-up

1. WARM-UP

Read a book about Groundhog Day or shadows. One example is *Groundhog Day* by Betsy Lewin (Aro Publishing Co., 1984). Discuss what a shadow is and how it is made. Explain the myth that if the groundhog sees his shadow, more winter weather is to come, and if he does not see his shadow, spring will arrive early.

2. VESTIBULAR

Teach the children the following chant:

> Groundhog, groundhog, oh so still.
> Will you come out?
> Yes, I will!

Have the children assume a squatting position while saying, "Groundhog, groundhog, oh so still. Will you come out?" When they say, "Yes, I will!," have them jump straight up. The children can take turns squatting inside a box (provide 2-3, if available), and pretend to jump up out of the "ground."

3. PROPRIOCEPTION

Use approximately 5 yards of tubular material to create a groundhog "tunnel." Have adults hold each end of the tunnel while the children pretend to be groundhogs and crawl through the tunnel. Repeat several times.

4. BALANCE

Teach the children about groundhog shadows. Turn off the lights and use a flashlight to demonstrate how to make a shadow. Tell the children they are going to pretend to be a shadow. Divide the children into partners and have them face each other. Have one partner balance on one leg then the other, hop on one foot then the other, and move slowly while the other partner pretends to be a shadow and follows along. Have the children switch roles.

5. EYE-HAND COORDINATION

While the children are sitting in a circle, turn off the light and have them follow a flashlight beam around the room. Tell them to watch and see the shadows.

6. COOL-DOWN

"I'm a Little Groundhog"
Sung to: "I'm a little Teapot"
(From www.preschooleducation.com; used with permission.)

I'm a little groundhog, (*Place hands on hips*)
Short and brown.
All winter long, (*Rest head on hands and pretend to sleep*)
I sleep underground.
On February 2nd (*Peek through cupped hands*)
I peek out and then,
If I see my shadow, (*Put hands over head as if hiding in a hole*)
I go in my hole again!

7. FINE MOTOR

Give each child green construction paper sized to wrap around a paper cup. Have them snip the paper on one edge to create grass and glue the paper "grass" around the outside of the paper cup. Then have the children glue a picture of a groundhog, copied from page 167, to a craft stick. Poke a hole in the bottom of the cup and slide the craft stick in. Let the children pretend the groundhog is popping out of the ground by sliding the stick up and down.

Materials
- *Groundhog Day* by Betsy Lewin (Aro Publishing Co., 1984)
- 2 boxes
- 5 yards of tubular material
- Flashlight
- Styrofoam cups – 1 for each child
- Green construction paper sized to wrap around a styrofoam cup – 1 for each child
- Glue, scissors
- Picture of a groundhog copied from page 167
- Craft sticks – 1 for each child

THEME: HiBERNATiNG BEARS

LESSON PLAN (QUiCK ViEW)

1. **Warm-Up:** Book: *Bear Snores On* by Karma Wilson and Jane Chapman
2. **Vestibular:** Bears' journey obstacle course
3. **Proprioception:** Musical bear hugs
4. **Balance:** Balance beam paper bear carry
5. **Eye-Hand Coordination:** Stuffed bear toss into "cave" box
6. **Cool-Down:** Hibernation song
7. **Fine Motor:** Paper cup bear cave

1. WARM-UP

Read a book about bears hibernating. *Bear Snores On* by Karma Wilson and Jane Chapman (Simon and Schuster Children's Publishing, 2002) is one example. Describe what hibernation is and talk about other animals that sleep in the winter.

2. VESTiBULAR

Set up an obstacle course in a circle using pillows or beanbag chairs to crawl over, a table to crawl under, and a tunnel to crawl through. Tape down white or brown bear paw prints between obstacles. Explain to the children how bears hibernate during the winter by sleeping in a cave. Tell the children that they have to crawl like a bear, on a long journey to get to the cave. Have the children move through the obstacle course and pretend to be bears.

The tunnel represents the "cave." Have the children perform a "bear walk"* when they see the paw prints. Repeat several times around.

3. PROPRiOCEPTiON

While the children are sitting in a circle, play music and have them pass around several large teddy bears. When the music stops, the children who are holding the bears hug and squeeze their teddy bear. The other children can give themselves a "bear" hug. Start the music again and repeat until all the children have had turns to hug a teddy bear.

4. BALANCE

Have the children walk on a balance beam several times carrying a paper bear (copy reproducible bear on page 168). On their last trip across the balance beam, they can place the bear into a pretend "cave" box.

5. EYE-HAND COORDINATION

Forming 2 groups, have the children take turns standing on a place marker and tossing 3 small bears into a box "cave."

6. COOL-DOWN

Have the children sing the following song.
Sung to: "Are You Sleeping?"
(From www.preschooleducation.com; used with permission.)

Bear is sleeping, Bear is sleeping
In a cave, in a cave.
I wonder when he'll come out,
I wonder when he'll come out.
In the spring, in the spring.

7. FINE MOTOR

Give each child a paper cup to serve as a cave. Have them glue cotton balls on the cup to represent snow on the cave. Then have them cut out a pre-drawn semi-circle from brown construction paper. Glue coffee grounds onto the semi-circle for dirt, then curl it up and place it in the paper cup. Finally, let the children place a small brown pom pom inside the cup to represent a bear.

Materials

- *Bear Snores On* by Karma Wilson and Jane Chapman (Simon and Schuster Children's Publishing, 2002)
- Tunnel
- Pillows or beanbag chair
- Table to crawl under
- White or brown paper bear paw prints
- Music
- Several large stuffed teddy bears
- Balance beam
- Brown construction paper bears – 1 for each child; copy from page 168
- Pretend small cave box for paper bears
- 2 place markers
- 6 small stuffed teddy bears
- 2 boxes
- Paper cups – 1 for each child
- Cotton balls
- Coffee grounds
- Brown construction paper with pre-drawn semi-circles
- Scissors, glue
- Brown pom poms – 1 for each child

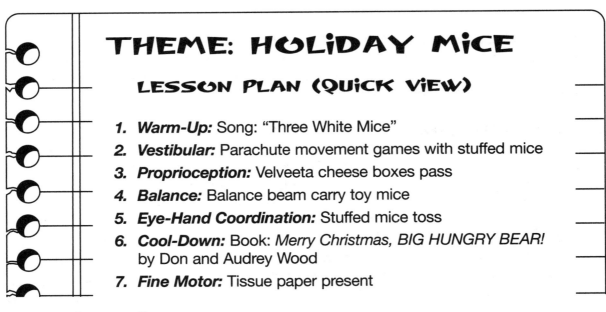

THEME: HOLIDAY MICE

LESSON PLAN (QUICK VIEW)

1. **Warm-Up:** Song: "Three White Mice"
2. **Vestibular:** Parachute movement games with stuffed mice
3. **Proprioception:** Velveeta cheese boxes pass
4. **Balance:** Balance beam carry toy mice
5. **Eye-Hand Coordination:** Stuffed mice toss
6. **Cool-Down:** Book: *Merry Christmas, BIG HUNGRY BEAR!* by Don and Audrey Wood
7. **Fine Motor:** Tissue paper present

1. WARM-UP

"Three White Mice"
Sung to: "Three Blind Mice"

> Three white mice, three white mice,
> See how they run, see how they run,
> They all ran after Santa Claus, they all ran after Santa Claus,
> To see if he left some presents,
> For three white mice.

2. VESTIBULAR

Have each child hold onto the edge of a parachute. Place several stuffed mice in the middle of the parachute. Have the children count how many mice there are. Explain that the mice have to help Santa's elves make toys for the holidays. The mice are going to ride on the parachute up to the North Pole, so they have to be careful that they do not fall off. Perform a variety of movement games with the parachute such as walking around in a circle in one direction, then the other, holding the parachute up high/down low, etc.

3. PROPRIOCEPTION

Collect 4 empty Velveeta or similar boxes, fill them with beanbags, and tape them closed. Explain to the children that they have to help feed cheese to the mice at the North Pole. Have the children sit in a circle. While playing holiday music (e.g., *The Nutcracker*), the children pass the boxes of cheese around the circle. When the music stops, the children stop passing the boxes. When the music resumes, the children pass the boxes in the opposite direction. Repeat until the end of the song.

4. BALANCE

Give each child a paper picture mouse, copied from the reproducible mouse on page 169. Have them walk across the balance beam carrying their mouse. Play holiday music in the background.

5. EYE-HAND COORDINATION

Place a bucket in the middle of the circle of children. Give each child a turn to toss 3 stuffed mice into the bucket. Each child stands up when it is his or her turn. Allow them to try until they make it.

6. COOL-DOWN

Read a book about mice celebrating holidays. *Merry Christmas, BIG HUNGRY BEAR!* by Don and Audrey Wood (The Blue Sky Press, 2002) is one example. Discuss why the mouse wanted to protect his gifts and what made him feel sad. Ask the children if they have ever felt sad, and if so, what made them sad.

7. FINE MOTOR

Give each child a copy of the reproducible drawing of a present on page 170. Have the children trace the square and plus sign for pre-writing skill practice. Then have them stick a bow in the center of the square. Finally, the children cut red/green tissue paper and glue onto the picture using a paintbrush. (Thin the glue with water.)

Materials

- Parachute or sheet
- At least 3 small stuffed mice for throwing
- Paper mice copied from the reproducible on page 169 – 1 for each child
- 4 empty Velveeta or similar-sized boxes filled with beanbags and taped closed
- Tape/CD *Nutcracker* ballet or other holiday music
- Balance beam
- Bucket
- *Merry Christmas, BIG HUNGRY BEAR* by Don and Audrey Wood (Blue Sky Press, 2002)
- Red/green tissue paper
- Thinned glue
- Paint brushes
- Reproducible picture of a present on page 170 – 1 for each child
- Peel-and-stick bows

THEME: HOLIDAY MUSIC

LESSON PLAN (QUICK VIEW)

1. **Warm-Up:** Song: "Jingle Bells" with props
2. **Vestibular:** Obstacle course with shakers (instruments)
3. **Proprioception:** "Little Drummer Boy" marching
4. **Balance:** Holiday musical dance and freeze balance game
5. **Eye Hand Coordination:** Passing presents fast and slow to holiday music
6. **Cool-Down:** Book: *Twelve Days of Christmas* by Jan Brett
7. **Fine Motor:** Paper plate holiday tambourines

1. WARM-UP
Give each child a bell for an instrumental prop. Have them sing the familiar holiday song "Jingle Bells."

2. VESTIBULAR
Set up an obstacle course using a variety of objects such as a balance beam, hula-hoops, objects to step over, a tunnel. Give each child a shaker. (These may be made by putting rice in recycled clear bottles or empty film containers. If using clear bottles, decorate the rice using red and/or green food coloring soaked in rubbing alcohol and left to dry overnight.) Show the children how to shake the shakers while moving through the obstacle course.

3. PROPRIOCEPTION
Show the children how to march slowly in place while stomping heavy feet to the beat of a drum. Then have children repeat. Use either a tape/CD of drumming or have an adult beat on a toy drum. Play "Little Drummer Boy" in the background.

4. BALANCE
Tell the children that they are going to play a musical balance game. Explain that holiday music will be playing and that they are to dance in place. When the music stops, instruct the children to perform a balance action, such as standing on one foot, hopping on one foot, and balancing with eyes closed.

5. EYE-HAND COORDINATION

(Prepare ahead of time 3 boxes wrapped in holiday paper. Fill 1 box with rice, 1 with beans, and 1 with dry noodles.) Have the children sit in a circle and pass the 3 wrapped boxes around the circle to the beat of holiday music. First play slow music, then fast, then slow, etc.

6. COOL-DOWN

Choose a holiday music book or read/sing the book *Twelve Days of Christmas* by Jan Brett (Trumpet Club, 1992). Discuss holidays around the world.

7. FINE MOTOR

Give each child a small-sized paper plate. Have the children punch a hole in the plate and show them how to thread a pipe cleaner through the hole. (Pre-attach a small silver or gold bell to a red or green pipe cleaner.) Let the children decorate the tambourine with colorful red and green ribbons attached with holiday stickers.

Materials

- Instrumental bells – 1 for each child
- Variety of obstacle course equipment (e.g., balance beam, hula-hoops, tunnel)
- Shakers made from recycled clear plastic containers or empty film containers filled with rice (the rice may be colored red or green by using several drops of red/green food coloring mixed with rubbing alcohol, soaked for 10-15 minutes, and allowed to dry overnight)
- Tape/CD of drumming or use a toy drum
- "Little Drummer Boy" music
- Tape/CD of holiday music for balance activity
- 3 wrapped boxes – 1 filled with rice, 1 with beans, 1 with dry noodles
- *Twelve Days of Christmas* by Jan Brett (Trumpet Club, 1992)
- Small-size paper plates – 1 for each child
- Hole punch (several)
- Red and green pipe cleaners cut in half (pre-thread a gold/silver bell onto pipe cleaner)
- Holiday stickers and red/green thin ribbon

THEME: HUMAN BODY

LESSON PLAN (QUICK VIEW)

1. **Warm-Up:** Song: "Head, Shoulders, Knees and Toes"
2. **Vestibular:** Song: "Hokey Pokey"
3. **Proprioception:** Theraband stretch
4. **Balance:** "Kid Connection" game
5. **Eye-Hand Coordination:** Tossing beanbag onto life-size body drawing
6. **Cool-Down: Book**: *Eyes, Nose, Fingers, and Toes* by Judy Hindley
7. **Fine Motor:** Paper person

1. WARM-UP

Sing the familiar song "Head, Shoulders, Knees and Toes" while performing the actions of touching the body parts with both hands as you name it.

Head, shoulders, knees and toes, knees and toes.
Head, shoulders, knees and toes, knees and toes, and
Eyes, and ears, and mouth, and nose.
Head, shoulders, knees and toes, knees and toes.

2. VESTIBULAR

Perform the traditional "Hokey Pokey" game. Have the children put in different body parts, including hips, ankles, knees, wrists, etc., both right and left.

3. PROPRIOCEPTION

Give each child a piece of theraband. Have them hold it in their hands and stretch it with their arms. Then have them put it under their foot and pick the foot up and push down, sit down with legs out straight and wrap it around their feet, then do sit-ups, etc. Label the body parts they are using as they perform each activity.

4. BALANCE

Play the "Kid Connection" game. Have the children stand with a partner. Call out body parts for the partners to touch together or connect. For example, "Back to back, hand to hand, foot to foot, knee to knee, elbow to elbow," etc.

5. EYE-HAND COORDINATION

Prepare ahead of time by drawing around a child's body on a large piece of bulletin board paper. (You may want 2 copies.) Tape the paper person to the floor. Have the children take turns tossing a beanbag onto the person and label the body part it landed on.

6. COOL-DOWN

Read a book about body parts. One example is *Eyes, Nose, Fingers, and Toes* by Judy Hindley (Candlewick Press, 1999). Have the children point to their own body parts when asked, such as "Where is your nose, ankles, elbows, wrists, knees," etc.

7. FINE MOTOR

Give each child an outline of a person. Have them draw eyes, nose, mouth, ears, and hair. Then have them glue fabric onto the outline to represent clothes.

Materials

- Theraband
- Large bulletin board paper drawn with life-sized outline of a child
- Beanbags
- *Eyes, Nose, Fingers, and Toes* by Judy Hindley (Candlewick Press, 1999)
- Small outline picture of a person – one for each child
- Crayons, glue, fabric pieces

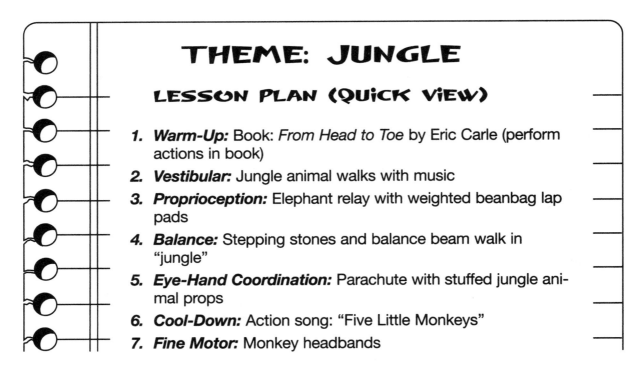

THEME: JUNGLE

LESSON PLAN (QUICK VIEW)

1. **Warm-Up:** Book: *From Head to Toe* by Eric Carle (perform actions in book)
2. **Vestibular:** Jungle animal walks with music
3. **Proprioception:** Elephant relay with weighted beanbag lap pads
4. **Balance:** Stepping stones and balance beam walk in "jungle"
5. **Eye-Hand Coordination:** Parachute with stuffed jungle animal props
6. **Cool-Down:** Action song: "Five Little Monkeys"
7. **Fine Motor:** Monkey headbands

1. WARM-UP

Read the book *From Head to Toe* by Eric Carle (HarperCollins Publishers, 1997). (The activities in this lesson plan relate directly to the story of the book.) Follow the actions described in the book. Discuss the types of animals found in the jungle.

2. VESTIBULAR

Have the children pretend to be different jungle animals and move around the room to "jungle" music. Elephant – children put arms together straight in front of them and swing arms back and forth. Monkey – children jump up and down while moving arms in an arc at sides. Lion/tiger – children crawl on hands and feet. Snake – children slither on their tummy on the floor.

3. PROPRIOCEPTION

Have the children pretend to be "heavy" elephants. They take a turn crawling on hands and knees across the room and around an object while carrying a weighted lap bag on their back. Have 2-3 children go at the same time in a relay and repeat for several turns.

4. BALANCE

Pretend to go into the jungle by crossing a creek. Place 6 stepping stones (purchased) and a balance beam on the floor in a line. Have the children count the number of stepping stones to reinforce number skills. With music playing, have the children walk on the stepping stones and across the balance beam. Gently spray a mist of "rainforest" water on the children when they reach the end of the balance beam. Repeat several turns.

5. EYE-HAND COORDINATION

Have the children each hold a handle on a parachute. Place several stuffed jungle animals in the center of the parachute. The children can watch the animals move around as they lift the parachute up and down, fast and slow, while walking in a circle in both directions, etc.

6. COOL-DOWN

Have the children sit in a circle and sing the following action song holding up the correct number of fingers as they count down the monkeys.
(From www.preschooleducation.com; original author unknown. Used with permission.)

> Five little monkeys high up in the tree
> Teasing Mr. Alligator.
> "You can't catch me, you can't catch me, you can't catch me."
> Along comes Mr. Alligator quiet as can be ...
> And SNAP that monkey right out of that tree!

Continue song until counting down to "Zero little monkeys ... along comes Mr. Alligator FAT as can be."

7. FINE MOTOR

Make a copy of the reproducible monkey's head on page 171 onto construction or tag board paper for each child. Have the children color and cut out the monkey head. Give the children crayons with the paper removed so that they can use the side of the crayon to color with. This will help develop finger grip strength. Staple the monkey head to a paper band to fit around the child's head.

Materials
- *From Head to Toe* by Eric Carle (HarperCollins Publishers, 1997)
- Jungle rhythm music
- 2-4 weighted lap bags (lap bags may be made by sewing together material filled with beans, rice, or corn in a size big enough to drape across a child's lap)
- Stepping stones
- Balance beam
- Tape/CD of jungle music
- Spray bottle filled with water
- Parachute
- Several stuffed jungle animals
- Picture of monkey head on page 171 copied onto tag board or construction paper – 1 per child
- Tag board "bands" to staple onto the monkey head – 1 per child
- Crayons, scissors, stapler

THEME: MiTTENS

LESSON PLAN (QUiCK VIEW)

1. **Warm-Up:** Book: *The Mitten* adapted and illustrated by Jan Brett
2. **Vestibular:** Parachute "mitten" game with puppet animal props
3. **Proprioception:** Sled pull (kid and stuffed animals)
4. **Balance:** Mitten match relay hopping on one foot
5. **Eye-Hand Coordination:** Ice bag toss/catch with mittens
6. **Cool-Down:** Pretend snow melting and snow angels
7. **Fine Motor:** Mitten color and lace

1. WARM-UP

Read the book *The Mitten* adapted and illustrated by Jan Brett (Scholastic, 1989). (The activities in this lesson plan relate directly to the story of the book.) Name the different animals that hide in the mitten. Explain why the boy's mitten was smaller than the other.

2. VESTiBULAR

Ahead of time, download from www.janbrett.com colored pictures of each of the animals from *The Mitten*. Cut them, glue to tag board, laminate them, and tape a tongue depressor on the back to create 8 puppets. To begin the activity, have the children sit on the floor and hold the parachute edges. Pass out the puppets to 8 children and have them crawl, one at a time, under the parachute pretending it is "The Mitten." Ask the 8 children to identify each of the animals. The other children continue to hold the parachute, moving it up and down to simulate the mitten opening, as the story depicts, when the bear sneezes. Repeat until all of the children have had turns with a puppet.

3. PROPRIOCEPTION

Have one child pull a "sled" while another child sits on the "sled" holding stuffed animals. (Choose animals that represent characters from the book.) The sled may be created from a cardboard box, or a scooter board may be used. A real plastic sled may also be used. Carpet squares may be used as sleds on a linoleum floor. Secure a rope to the sled for pulling or have the child push from behind. If there is space in the classroom, two sleds may be used at the same time to allow children more turns.

4. BALANCE

Divide the children into 2 relay teams. Give each child one mitten and place the matching pair at the other end of the room. The mittens may be real or made of paper. Be sure to create a matching pattern on each pair of paper mittens. Have one child from each team hop on one foot to the other side of the room and find the matching mitten, then hop on one foot back. Have all the children take turns. Give each child a different mitten to match and repeat. Ask the children to describe what their mittens look like (e.g., color, size, shape).

5. EYE-HAND COORDINATION
Divide the children into partners. Have them toss a bag filled with ice back and forth. Be sure the children wear mittens or socks on their hands.

6. COOL-DOWN
Have the children relax and pretend to be snow melting. They begin by standing up and then slowly lowering themselves to the ground to lie down. Have them pretend to make snow angels by lying on their backs and moving their arms and legs out to the side against the floor.

7. FINE MOTOR
Download the black-and-white coloring picture of "The Mitten" (includes all of the animals) from www.janbrett.com. You will need 1 for each child. Prepare ahead of time by cutting around the outside of the picture, glue to tag board, punch holes around the edge of the picture, and tie a string in one of the holes. It is easier for the children to lace through the holes if tape is wrapped around one end of the string. Have the children color the picture and then lace the string through every hole.

Materials
- *The Mitten* adapted and illustrated by Jan Brett (Scholastic, 1989)
- Parachute
- Mitten character puppets downloaded in color from www.janbrett.com. Cut, glue to tag board, laminate, tape on tongue depressor to each animal
- Stuffed animal characters from the book
- 1-2 sleds: Choose between boxes, carpet squares, scooter boards, or real plastic sleds; rope optional
- Plastic bags filled with ice
- Mittens, gloves, or socks for children to wear
- Matching mittens, either real or of paper, for balance activity – at least 1 pair for each child
- Black-and-white coloring picture of "The Mitten" with animals inside – 1 for each child (download from www.janbrett.com). Prepare ahead of time by cutting, gluing to tag board, punching holes around the outside edge, tying a string in one hole and securing tape on the other side of the string for lacing
- Crayons

THEME: MOTHER'S DAY

LESSON PLAN (QUICK VIEW)

1. **Warm-Up:** Book: *Are You My Mother?* by P. D. Eastman
2. **Vestibular:** Obstacle course to "pick" flowers
3. **Proprioception:** Therapy ball "back rubs"
4. **Balance:** "Mother, May I?" balance game
5. **Eye-Hand Coordination:** "Sorting laundry" beanbag toss
6. **Cool-Down:** Song: "I Love My Mommy"
7. **Fine Motor:** Paper flower bouquet

1. WARM-UP

Read a book about mothers. One example is *Are You My Mother?* by P. D. Eastman (Random House, 1960). Explain that some mommies are grandmas, some are step-moms, some are foster moms, etc. Have the children each give an example of how their mommy cares for them.

2. VESTIBULAR

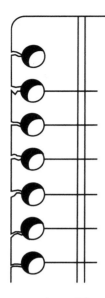

Set up an obstacle course using a variety of objects such as a tunnel to crawl through, hula-hoops to jump in/out of, stepping stones to walk on, etc. Place construction paper flowers along the path. Explain to the children that on Mother's Day, moms like to receive flowers. Have the children move through the obstacle course several times. Along the way, call out a child's name and have him/her pick up a flower for mommy (they may be asked to identify the color as well).

3. PROPRIOCEPTION

Explain that moms sometimes give back rubs to help their children relax and fall asleep. Have all of the children lie on their tummies and roll a therapy ball across their backs.

4. BALANCE

Play the traditional children's game "Mother, May I?" Have one child be the mother (wearing a scarf around his/her neck as a prop) and stand at one end of the room; the other children stand in a row facing the "mother." The children say in unison, "Mother, may I …" while an adult finishes the sentence with a balance task such as "… stand on one foot?, hop on one foot?, walk heel to toe, walk backward heel to toe, etc." The mother answers "Yes, you may," and the children perform the balance task.

5. EYE-HAND COORDINATION

Explain to the children that moms do a lot of housework; one chore they often do is laundry. Divide the children into 2 groups and have them pretend to sort laundry by tossing 3 beanbags into a laundry basket.

6. COOL-DOWN

"I Love Mommy"
Sung to: "Are You Sleeping?"
(From www.preschooleducation.com; original author unknown. Used with permission.)

> I love mommy, I love mommy.
> Yes I do; yes I do.
> And my mommy loves me,
> Yes, my mommy loves me,
> Loves me too; loves me too.

7. FINE MOTOR

Give each child an 11x14" piece of green construction paper folded in half lengthwise, with cutting lines drawn perpendicular along the folded side 1" apart, and stopping about 1-2" from the open edge. Have the children cut along the lines, stopping where they end. Separate the two open ends, sliding the paper so that the open ends are staggered about 1" apart, then staple in place (this will cause the cut strips to loop). Next, roll the paper into a "bouquet" so that the flat edge of the loops are on the outside, and staple together. This will form the stems for the flowers. Have the children cut pictures of flowers out of magazines and glue a flower picture at the end of each "stem."

Materials

- *Are You My Mother?* by P. D. Eastman (Random House, 1960)
- Obstacle course equipment such as a tunnel, stepping stones, hula-hoops, etc.
- 1-3 large therapy balls
- Construction paper flowers – 1 for each child
- 2 laundry baskets
- 6 beanbags
- 2 spot markers
- Scarf
- 11x14" piece of green construction paper folded in half lengthwise with cutting lines drawn along the folded side of the construction paper 1" apart, and stopping about 1-2" from the edge
- Magazines with pictures of flowers
- Scissors, glue, stapler

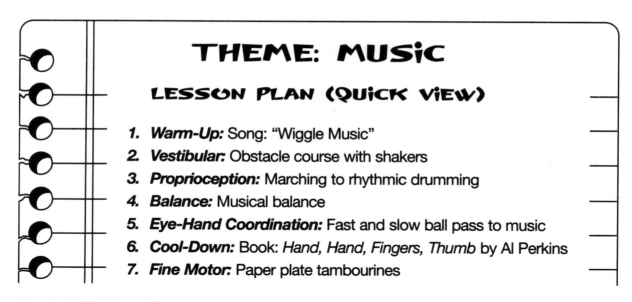

THEME: MUSIC

LESSON PLAN (QUICK VIEW)

1. **Warm-Up:** Song: "Wiggle Music"
2. **Vestibular:** Obstacle course with shakers
3. **Proprioception:** Marching to rhythmic drumming
4. **Balance:** Musical balance
5. **Eye-Hand Coordination:** Fast and slow ball pass to music
6. **Cool-Down:** Book: *Hand, Hand, Fingers, Thumb* by Al Perkins
7. **Fine Motor:** Paper plate tambourines

1. WARM-UP

"Wiggle Music"
Sung to: "The Bear Went over the Mountain"
(Adapted from preschooleducation.com; original author unknown. Used with permission.)

Have the children rhythmically shake each body part as it is named in the song.
Oh, my hands are starting to wiggle,
My hands are starting to wiggle,
My hands are starting to wiggle,
And So is the rest of me!
(Repeat using different body parts... arms, feet, legs, fingers, thumbs.)

2. VESTIBULAR

Set up an obstacle course using a variety of objects such as a balance beam, hula-hoops, objects to step over, tunnel, etc. Give each child a shaker. (May be made using rice in recycled plastic bottles or empty film containers.) Show the children how to shake the shakers making their own music and rhythm, while moving through the obstacle course.

3. PROPRIOCEPTION

Show the children how to march slowly in place with heavy feet to the beat of a drum. Use either a tape/CD of drumming or have an adult beat on a toy or real drum.

4. BALANCE

Tell the children that they are going to play a musical balance game. Explain that music will be playing and that they are to dance in place. When the music stops, instruct the children to perform a balance action, such as standing on one foot, hopping on one foot, and balancing with eyes closed.

5. EYE-HAND COORDINATION

Have the children sit in a circle. Pass 3 balls of different sizes and weights (ask the children to identify which ball is smallest/largest) around the circle to the beat of music. First play slow music, then fast, then slow, etc.

6. COOL-DOWN

Read a book about music. *Hand, Hand, Finger, Thumb* by Al Perkins, illustrated by Eric Gurney (Random House, 1969), is one example. Have the children pretend to drum, using their hands on their laps, along with the book when it reads "drumming on drums."

7. FINE MOTOR

Give each child a small-sized paper plate. Have them punch a hole in the plate and thread a pipe cleaner through the hole. (Pre-attach a small silver or gold bell to the pipe cleaner.) Help them twist it closed. Let the children decorate the tambourine with colorful ribbons attached with stickers.

Materials

- A variety of obstacle course equipment (e.g., balance beam, hula-hoops, tunnel)
- Shakers made from recycled plastic containers or empty film containers filled with rice or beans
- Tape/CD of drumming or use a toy or real drum
- Tape/CD of any variety of music for balance activity
- 3 balls of different sizes and weights
- *Hand, Hand, Fingers, Thumb* by Al Perkins, illustrated by Eric Gurney (Random House, 1969)
- Small-size paper plates – 1 for each child
- Hole punch (several)
- Pipe cleaners approximately 6" long (pre-thread a gold/silver bell onto pipe cleaner)
- Stickers and colorful, thin ribbon

THEME: NUMBERS

LESSON PLAN (QUICK VIEW)

1. **Warm-Up:** Song: "Ten Little Indians" – substitute fingers, hearts, apples, etc.
2. **Vestibular:** Obstacle course (stepping stones, hula-hoops, paper numbers)
3. **Proprioception:** "Simon Says" number game
4. **Balance:** Jump rope forming numbers
5. **Eye-Hand Coordination:** Bubbles – Counting how many bubbles children can pop
6. **Cool-Down:** Book: *Over in the Meadow* by Olive A. Wadsworth and David Carter
7. **Fine Motor:** Peanut butter dough – form numbers ... eat!

1. WARM-UP

Have the children sing the familiar tune of "Ten Little Indians." Substitute objects. For example, the children can sing "10 little fingers" and hold up each finger as they count to 10. Or a flannel board may be used, and the children could sing and count a variety of felt objects placed on the flannel board such as hearts, apples, or even numbers.

2. VESTIBULAR

Set up an obstacle course in a circle with a variety of equipment items to move on, through, and around. For example, ask the children to count the number of stepping stones as they walk on them, count the number of jumps they need to hop into hula-hoops placed in a row, and identify paper numbers taped to the floor as they bear walk* over them.

3. PROPRIOCEPTION

Have the children play a game of "Simon Says." Hold up a card with a number on it and have the children identify it. Then instruct the children to perform a "heavy work" task the number of times shown on the card. Examples include: clap hands 5 times, stomp on the ground 7 times, stand up/sit down 3 times, slap legs 6 times, push hands together 4 times, etc.

4. BALANCE

Divide the children into small groups and give each group a jump rope. Show the children how to form different numbers on the floor using the jump rope. Then have them walk heel to toe on the jump rope "number." Repeat for several different numbers.

5. EYE-HAND COORDINATION

Have the children sit in a circle. When it is their turn, point to them or lightly touch them on the head so they know when to stand up. Blow bubbles to the child standing, and have the other children count how many bubbles their friend can pop. Repeat until all the children have had a turn standing up.

6. COOL-DOWN

Read a book about counting numbers. One example is *Over in the Meadow* by Olive A. Wadsworth and David Carter. Have the children imitate the different sounds and movements of each creature in the book.

7. FINE MOTOR

Have the children help make peanut butter dough.

Recipe

Combine the following ingredients:
2 cups honey
2 cups peanut butter (substitute almond butter for children allergic to peanut butter)
4 cups nonfat dried milk (for children allergic to milk, substitute dehydrated soy milk)

Encourage the children to play with the dough – pinching, pulling, kneading, and finally rolling it into a snake. Give each child a paper plate with a large-sized number drawn on it and have them form the "snake" dough over the number. Repeat for several numbers, and then enjoy eating! Great sensory experience – tactile, olfactory, and gustatory as well as oral motor skill development.

Materials

- Stepping stones
- Hula-hoops
- Paper numbers taped to the floor
- Cards with numbers
- 3-4 jump ropes
- Bubbles
- *Over in the Meadow* by Olive A. Wadsworth and David Carter (Scholastic, 1992)
- 2 cups honey, 2 cups peanut butter, 4 cups nonfat dried milk (see note above)
- Mixing bowl and spoon
- Paper plates with large-sized numbers written on them

THEME: NURSERY RHYMES
LESSON PLAN (QUICK VIEW)

1. **Warm-Up:** Book: *To Market, To Market* by Anne Miranda
2. **Vestibular:** "Jack Be Nimble" (jump over candlestick)
3. **Proprioception:** "Shear the Sheep" activity
4. **Balance:** "Twinkle, Twinkle, Little Star" balance game
5. **Eye-Hand Coordination:** "Mary Had a Little Lamb" catch/throw
6. **Cool-Down:** Song: "To Rhyming Land We Go"
7. **Fine Motor:** Necklace with straws and "Little Star"

1. WARM-UP

Read the book *To Market, To Market* by Anne Miranda, illustrated by Janet Stevens (Harcourt Inc., 1997), or a similar book about animals. Talk about how the animals do silly things in the book. Have the children help describe these actions by asking "What is this animal doing?"

2. VESTIBULAR

Have the children recite the nursery rhyme "Jack Be Nimble, Jack Be Quick."

> Jack be nimble.
> Jack be quick.
> Jack jump over the candlestick.

Set up 2 candlesticks across the room from where the children are sitting. Divide the children into 2 groups for a relay. Have 2 children at a time run and jump over the candlesticks, then back to the group so 2 more children can take a turn. Repeat until everyone has had several turns. Monitor group activity level to see if it is necessary to discontinue activity.

3. PROPRIOCEPTION

Have the children recite the nursery rhyme "Baa, Baa, Black Sheep."

> Baa baa black sheep have you any wool?
> Yes Sir, yes Sir, three bags full.
> One for my master, one for my dame,
> and one for the little boy who lives down the lane.

Have the children practice counting to 3. Divide the children into partners. Have them pretend to "sheer" the sheep. One child assumes hands-on-knees position* while the other uses a beanbag to pretend sheer by pushing on the partner's back and down his or her arms and legs. Switch partners and repeat.

4. BALANCE

Have the children recite the nursery rhyme "Twinkle, Twinkle Little Star."

Twinkle, twinkle, little star.
How I wonder what you are.
Up above the world so high.
Like a diamond in the sky.
Twinkle, twinkle, little star.
How I wonder what you are.

Pre-cut paper stars (copy reproducible star on page 172), write each child's name on a star, and place it on the floor in front of the child. Give directions to the children such as stand on one foot on the star; hop over the star; jump backward onto the star; etc.

5. EYE-HAND COORDINATION
Sing the nursery rhyme "Mary Had a Little Lamb."

Mary had a little lamb, little lamb, little lamb.
Mary had a little lamb.
Whose fleece was white as snow.

Divide children into 2-3 small groups and have them throw and catch small stuffed lambs to each other. They can count how many times they catch the lambs.

6. COOL-DOWN
Teach the children the following song.
"To Rhyming Land We Go"
Sung to: "Farmer in the Dell"
(From www.preschooleducation.com; original author unknown. Used with permission.)

To rhyming land we go, to rhyming land we go,
Hi Ho the dairy oh.
To rhyming land we go.

Then recite these verses repeating as above:
Jack and Jill fell down ...
Bo Peep has lost her sheep ...
Boy Blue is fast asleep ...
The cat can play a tune ...
The cow jumps over the moon ...
A star shines in the sky ...
And now we'll say goodbye ...!

7. FINE MOTOR
Have the children cut straws into approximately 1-inch pieces and lace them onto yarn. Next, have them spread glue onto a paper star and sprinkle it with glitter. (Use the stars from the balance game; be sure to punch a hole in the star.) Finally, have the children lace the star on to the yarn and wear the necklace.

Materials
- *To Market, To Market* by Anne Miranda (Harcourt Inc., 1997)
- 2-3 candlesticks
- Beanbags
- Yellow paper stars for balance game and for fine-motor activity – 1 for each child; copy from page 172
- 3-4 small stuffed animal lambs
- Straws, glue, glitter, scissors

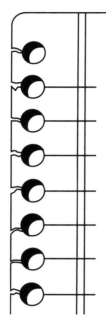

THEME: NUTRITION/FOOD

LESSON PLAN (QUICK VIEW)

1. **Warm-Up:** Songs: "Picked a Strawberry and "Peanut Butter and Jelly"
2. **Vestibular:** Grocery store obstacle course to match pictures
3. **Proprioception:** "Kid" peanut butter and jelly sandwiches
4. **Balance:** "Balancing Diet"
5. **Eye-Hand Coordination:** Beanbag fruit/vegetable toss into "grocery cart"
6. **Cool-Down:** Book: *Jamberry* by Bruce Degen
7. **Fine motor:** Scented strawberry paint

1. WARM-UP

Song "Picked a Strawberry"
Sung to: "Clementine"
(From www.preschooleducation.com original author unknown. Used with permission.))

Picked a strawberry,
Picked a strawberry
That was growing in the sun,
Then I washed it,
Then I ate it,
Then I picked another one.

Action chant "Peanut Butter and Jelly."
Perform actions appropriate for the action words.

Peanut butter, peanut butter, and jelly, and jelly (refrain)
First you take the dough and knead it, knead it.
  (Push heels of hands together – refrain)
Pop it in the oven and bake it, bake it.
  (Extend arms toward "oven" – refrain)
Then you take a knife and slice it, slice it.
  ("Saw" back and forth with side of hand – refrain)
Then you take some peanuts and crack them, crack them.
  (Pound fists together – refrain)
Put them on the floor and mash them, mash them.
  (Push fist into palm of other hand – refrain)
Then you take a knife and spread it, spread it.
  (Brush palms together for spreading – refrain)
Next you take some grapes and squash them, squash them. *(Stamp feet – refrain)*
Glop it on the bread and smear it, smear it. *(Repeat spreading motion again – refrain)*
Then you take the sandwich and eat it, eat it.
  (Open/close mouth as if biting – refrain)

98 Learn to Move, Move to Learn!

2. VESTIBULAR

Tell the children they are going to the grocery store to buy some vegetables. Set up an obstacle course using a variety of props such as a balance beam, tunnel, objects to step over, etc. Give each child a picture of a vegetable from magazines. When the children get to the end of the obstacle course, have them find the matching vegetable at the "grocery store." Lay out the pictures on a table so the children can match them.

3. PROPRIOCEPTION

Divide the children into partners. Have one child lie face down on the floor, while the other child pretends to spread peanut butter, then jelly, on the partner's back. Be sure they use flat hands with firm pressure. Switch partners.

4. BALANCE

Each child holds a plastic fruit or vegetable "prop" – 1 in each hand. Then he/she balances on a balance board or on one foot. Teach the children about the importance of balanced healthy foods.

5. EYE-HAND COORDINATION

Have the children take turns tossing pretend fruits/vegetables into a pretend "grocery cart" basket using beanbags. The children can name the color of each beanbag and think of a fruit/vegetable that is the same color.

6. COOL DOWN

Read a book about food. *Jamberry* by Bruce Degen (Harper Trophy, 1983) is one example. Ask the children to name the different fruits introduced in the book. Have the children taste each fruit by providing some samples (blueberries, strawberries, blackberries, raspberries).

7. FINE MOTOR

Copy the picture of the reproducible strawberry on page 173 – 1 for each child. Mix dry strawberry Jello or dry strawberry Kool-aid with wet red tempera paint. Using paintbrushes, the children paint their strawberry picture. This makes a nice olfactory sensory experience! Using a Q-tip, let them pain on black "seeds."

Materials

- Obstacle course props such as balance beam, tunnel, objects to step over
- Magazine pictures of vegetables and fruits (cut out 2 matching pictures)
- Plastic fruits and vegetables
- Balance boards 2-3 (optional)
- Beanbags
- Baskets (at least 2)
- *Jamberry* by Bruce Degen (Harper Trophy, 1983)
- Fruit samples (blueberries, strawberries, blackberries, raspberries)
- Drawing of a strawberry on page 173 – 1 for each child
- Red tempera paint
- Paint brushes
- Dry strawberry Jello or Kool-aid mix
- Q-tips
- Black tempera paint

THEME: OCEAN/BEACH

LESSON PLAN (QUICK VIEW)

1. **Warm-Up:** Song: "Waves at the Beach"
2. **Vestibular:** Crab walk and fish swim
3. **Proprioception:** Snorkeling with straws
4. **Balance:** "Fish out of water"
5. **Eye-Hand Coordination:** Magnet fishing
6. **Cool-Down:** Book: *Out of the Ocean* by Debra Frasier
7. **Fine Motor:** Paper plate ocean scene

1. WARM-UP

"Waves at the Beach"
Sung to "Wheels on the Bus"
(From www.preschooleducation.com submitted by Louise Dawson; printed with permission.)

> The waves at the beach go up and down, up and down, up and down,
>   the waves at the beach go up and down, all day long.
> The crabs at the beach crawl back and forth, back and forth, back and forth,
> The crabs at the beach crawl back and forth, all day long.
> The lobsters at the beach go, snap, snap, snap; snap, snap, snap; snap, snap, snap
> The lobsters at the beach go snap, snap, snap, all day long
> The clams at the beach will open and shut, open and shut, open and shut,
> The clams at the beach will open and shut, all day long.
> The jelly fish go wibble, wobble, wibble; wibble, wobble, wibble, wibble, wobble, wibble,
>   wibble,
> The jelly fish go wibble, wobble, wibble, all day long.

2. VESTIBULAR

Have the children pretend to be crabs and "crab walk"* around the room. Then have them pretend to be fish in the ocean and "swim" around the room with their tummies on the floor. (Optional: Play ocean waves music in the background.)

3. PROPRIOCEPTION

(From www.preschooleducation.com; used with permission.)
Underneath a table, tape various pictures of ocean life. Drape a blanket or a sheet over the table. The children use bendable straws as snorkels and enter the water (crawl under the table) in small groups because you should never snorkel alone. Allow the group one minute in the "water." When they come out, ask questions about what they saw.

4. BALANCE

Have the children sit in a circle. Give each child a paper fish (copy reproducible fish on page 174). Similar to playing "Duck, Duck, Goose," have one child be "it" and touch each child's head saying "fish, fish, fish out of water." The child who is "it" stands up and chases the other child around the circle. The children move by walking backwards and pretend swim using their arms for fins.

5. EYE-HAND COORDINATION

Keep the children in a circle formation. Place the paper fish on the floor in the middle of the circle. (Be sure each paper fish has a paper clip attached.) Have the children use home-made fishing poles (with a magnet attached to the end of the string) and take turns catching the paper fish.

6. COOL-DOWN

Read a book about oceans and beaches. One example is *Out of the Ocean* by Debra Frasier (Scholastic, 1998). Discuss parts of the ocean such as seashells, sand, seaweed, and buried treasures.

7. FINE MOTOR

Have the children create an underwater ocean scene. Have each child place several fish stickers on a paper plate. Then have them tear green tissue paper (seaweed) and glue onto the paper plate. Finally, give each child a piece of blue plastic wrap to wrap around the paper plate.

Materials

- (Optional: Ocean waves music)
- Table with pictures of ocean life taped underneath
- Blanket/sheet draped over the table
- Bendable straws – 1 for each child
- Paper fish with paper clips attached to each one –
  copy 1 for each child from page 174
- 2-3 home-made fishing poles (sticks with string and magnets attached)
- *Out of the Ocean* by Debra Frasier (Scholastic, 1998)
- Paper plates – 1 for each child
- Fish stickers
- Green tissue paper
- Glue
- Blue plastic wrap

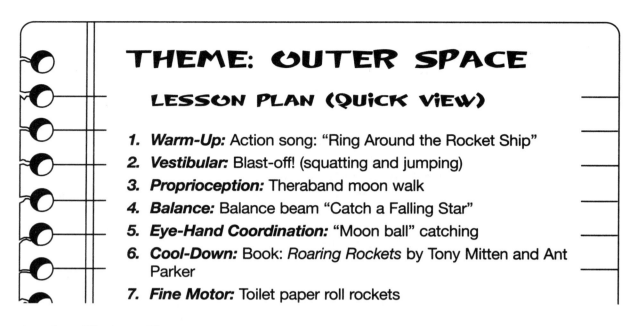

THEME: OUTER SPACE

LESSON PLAN (QUICK VIEW)

1. **Warm-Up:** Action song: "Ring Around the Rocket Ship"
2. **Vestibular:** Blast-off! (squatting and jumping)
3. **Proprioception:** Theraband moon walk
4. **Balance:** Balance beam "Catch a Falling Star"
5. **Eye-Hand Coordination:** "Moon ball" catching
6. **Cool-Down:** Book: *Roaring Rockets* by Tony Mitten and Ant Parker
7. **Fine Motor:** Toilet paper roll rockets

1. WARM-UP

"Ring Around the Rocket Ship"
Sung to: "Ring Around the Roses"
Have the children stand in a circle. Repeat several times.

> Ring around the rocket ship, (*Turn around*)
> Try to catch a star. (*Reach with hand*)
> Star dust, star dust, (*Wiggle fingers*)
> Fall where you are. (*Sit down*)

2. VESTIBULAR

Have the children pretend to be rockets. To do so, they squat, count backward from 10, then yell "blast-off!" and jump up as high as they can. Repeat several times.

3. PROPRIOCEPTION

Give each child a piece of theraband that is tied together at the ends to form a circle. Tell them that they are going to go for a walk on the moon. Have them put the theraband around their ankles and walk around the room. Play space music in the background.

4. BALANCE

Set up a balance beam with paper stars (copy reproducible star on page 172) next to the beam on either side. Have the children take turns walking across the balance beam and squatting to pick up a star off the floor. Repeat several times.

5. EYE-HAND COORDINATION

Make several "moon balls" by wadding large pieces of aluminum foil into a ball shape. Divide the children into several small groups. Have them throw and catch the "moon balls."

6. COOL-DOWN

Read a book about space. One example is *Roaring Rockets* by Tony Mitten and Ant Parker (Scholastic, 1997). Name different planets in space (e.g., moon, earth, Mars, Jupiter, Saturn, Venus, etc.). Talk about astronauts, stars, and rockets.

7. FINE MOTOR

Prepare ahead of time by taping an egg carton cup onto one side of a toilet paper roll, 1 for each child. (This will make a rocket model.) Have the children glue small pieces of aluminum foil and place star stickers around the rocket. Finally, have the children glue crepe paper streamer strips to the bottom of the rocket for pretend flames.

Materials

- Theraband tied into loops – 1 for each child
- Balance beam
- Paper stars; copy from page 172
- Large pieces of aluminum foil formed into "moon balls"
- *Roaring Rockets* by Tony Mitten and Ant Parker (Scholastic, 1997)
- Toilet paper tubes with egg carton cups taped to one end – 1 for each child
- Small square pieces of aluminum foil
- Star stickers
- Orange and red crepe paper streamers cut into 3" strips – several for each child
- Glue put into milk jug lids
- Q-tips to dip in glue

THEME: PETE'S A PIZZA

LESSON PLAN (QUICK VIEW)

1. **Warm-Up:** Book: *Pete's a Pizza* by William Steig
2. **Vestibular:** Log rolling on a mat "twirling" the dough
3. **Proprioception:** Partner pizza making
4. **Balance:** Supine flexion pretend baking
5. **Eye-Hand Coordination:** Beanbag pizza toss
6. **Cool-Down:** "Pizza Man" action poem
7. **Fine Motor:** Paper pizza

1. WARM-UP

Read the book *Pete's a Pizza* by William Steig (HarperCollins Publishers/Scholastic, 1998). (The activities in this lesson plan relate directly to the story of the book.) Discuss the shape of a whole pizza versus a slice of pizza.

2. VESTIBULAR

Have the children take turns log rolling* up/down a mat pretending to be twirling pizza dough.

3. PROPRIOCEPTION

Divide the children into partners. One child lies down on her stomach while the partner, using two open hands, gently pushes on her back, legs, and arms. After "kneading the dough," have the child apply lotion and sprinkle baby powder to exposed arms (pretend oil and flour), and then place checkers and shredded yellow paper on the partner's back (pretend pepperoni and cheese).

4. BALANCE

While keeping the same partners, have one child assume a supine flexion posture* (pretending to be baking in the oven). The other child counts to 10 while the partner "bakes." Then the child gently pokes the partner, on a shoulder or knee, with a finger to test and see if the pizza is "done."

5. EYE-HAND COORDINATION

Keeping the same partners, give each pair a beanbag. Explain that they are tossing pizza dough in the air and have them play catch back and forth with the beanbag. Have them count how many times they can catch the "dough."

6. COOL-DOWN

"Pizza Man" action poem
(From www.preschooleducation.com; original author unknown. Used with permission.)

> Pat a cake, pat a cake, pizza man.
> Make me a pizza as fast as you can!
> Roll it and toss it and sprinkle it with cheese.
> And don't forget 5 pepperonis, please!

7. FINE MOTOR

Give each child a paper plate with lines drawn on it to look like a slice of pizza. Have the children color the plate using a red crayon. Take the paper off the outside of the crayons, and have the children use the side of the crayon by rubbing it to color. The children cut out the piece of pizza. Then they glue the following to the paper plate: small green construction paper squares ("green peppers") small red construction paper circles ("pepperoni"), small yellow construction paper rectangles ("cheese"), and small white construction paper triangles ("onions"). Have the children name the shapes and colors of the toppings.

Materials

- *Pete's a Pizza* by William Steig (HarperCollins/Scholastic, 1998)
- Mat
- Lotion
- Baby powder
- Checkers
- Shredded yellow paper
- Beanbags
- Paper plates (with a triangle "slice of pizza" drawn on it)
- Green construction paper squares (pretend green peppers)
- Red construction paper circles (pretend pepperoni)
- Yellow construction paper rectangles (pretend cheese)
- White construction paper triangles (pretend onions)
- Red crayons with the paper removed
- Glue and scissors

THEME: PETS

LESSON PLAN (QUICK VIEW)

1. **Warm-Up:** Dog and cat warm-up exercises
2. **Vestibular:** Dog tricks – rolling, knee walking, crawling
3. **Proprioception:** Rope tug
4. **Balance:** Balance beam – feed the dog a bone
5. **Eye-Hand Coordination:** Cat "batting"
6. **Cool-Down:** Book: *Cookie's Week* by Cindy Ward
7. **Fine Motor:** Paper bag cat/dog puppet

1. WARM-UP

Have the children perform a variety of dog-and-cat exercises. Assume a hands-and-feet position* and stretch like a cat. While on hands and knees, children do a dog crawl* pretending to be a dog shaking off water. Swinging their head side to side, children pretend to wiggle dog ears. Have them clap "paws" together. Lastly, have them meow like a cat and bark like a dog. (Kids love this!)

2. VESTIBULAR

Tell the children they are going to pretend to be dogs performing tricks. Use a mat for the activities. First, the children roll on the mat one way, then the other. On the second turn, they pretend to "beg like a dog" by knee walking* across the mat. And on the last turn, they crawl like a dog or cat across the mat.

3. PROPRIOCEPTION

Explain to the children that dogs love to play "tug on a rope" games. A dog uses his teeth, but the children are going to use their hands. Divide the children into 2 groups and have the groups face each other while playing tug-of-war with a rope. Sustain the pull for a few seconds, and then let the children rest. Repeat several times.

4. BALANCE

Create a small doghouse from a cardboard box and place a stuffed animal dog inside. Position this at the end of a balance beam. Give each child a pretend dog bone (purchased or made of construction paper). Have the children walk across a balance beam while carrying the dog bone. After they step off the balance beam, have them place their dog bone next to the stuffed animal dog inside his doghouse.

5. EYE-HAND COORDINATION

Tie a small object representing a cat toy to the end of a string and hang it from the ceiling just high enough for a child to jump up and touch it. (You may want to make several of them and place them around the room.) Explain to the children that cats love to "bat" at string. Have the children take turns pretending to be a cat batting at the string hanging from the ceiling. They stand under the string and coordinate their eyes and hands to jump up and touch the "cat toy" on the string.

6. COOL-DOWN

Read a book about pets. One example is *Cookie's Week* by Cindy Ward, illustrated by Tomie dePaola (Scholastic, 1988). Ask the children if they have a pet at home and whether it is a cat, dog, bird, turtle, etc. Ask what they do to take care of their pet, such as giving it food and water and playing with it.

7. FINE MOTOR

Allow the children to choose either the cat or dog reproducible paper bag cut-outs on pages 175-176. Have them color, cut, and glue the cat or dog onto a paper bag. Use pipe cleaners for whiskers, and cut out triangles for ears to glue to the top of the cat or dog head.

Materials

- Mat
- Long rope
- Small doghouse made out of a cardboard box
- Stuffed animal dog
- Dog bones (purchased or made of construction paper)
- Balance beam
- 2-3 pieces of string with a small object representing a cat toy tied to the ends
- *Cookie's Week* by Cindy Ward, illustrated by Tomie dePaola (Scholastic, 1988)
- Cat or dog reproducible paper bag puppet pattern on pages 175-176
- Paper bags – 1 for each child
- Pipe cleaners, construction paper triangle ears
- Scissors, glue, crayons

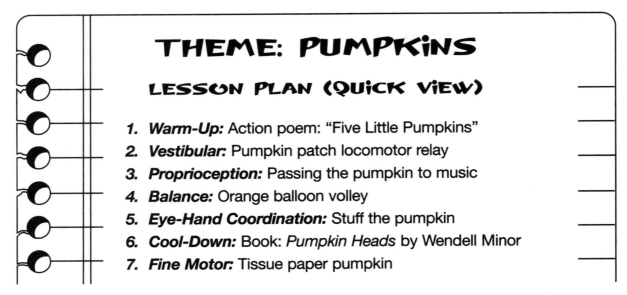

THEME: PUMPKINS

LESSON PLAN (QUICK VIEW)

1. **Warm-Up:** Action poem: "Five Little Pumpkins"
2. **Vestibular:** Pumpkin patch locomotor relay
3. **Proprioception:** Passing the pumpkin to music
4. **Balance:** Orange balloon volley
5. **Eye-Hand Coordination:** Stuff the pumpkin
6. **Cool-Down:** Book: *Pumpkin Heads* by Wendell Minor
7. **Fine Motor:** Tissue paper pumpkin

1. WARM-UP

Action Poem: "Five Little Pumpkins"
(From www.preschooleducation.com; original author unknown. Used with permission.)

Optional: This warm-up activity may also be performed using a flannel board. Simply cut out 5 orange felt pumpkins and a brown felt gate and place them on a flannel board. The children can participate by helping to count the pumpkins. In addition, the teacher can discuss prepositions of "on, under, beside" the gate. Perform the actions designated in the parentheses while saying the words:

Five little pumpkins (*One hand up*)
Sitting on a gate.
The first one said, (*Point to thumb*)
"My, it's getting late."
The second one said, (*Pointer finger*)
"There are witches in the air."
The third one said, (*Middle finger*)
"But we don't care."
The fourth one said, (*Ring finger*)
"We'll run and run and run."
The fifth one said, (*Little finger*)
"It's just Halloween fun."
"Whoooooo" went the wind
And out went the light, (*Clap hands*)
And the five little pumpkins rolled out of sight.
(*Roll arms*)

2. VESTIBULAR

Copy about 12 pumpkins of the reproducible pumpkin on page 177 onto orange construction paper. Cut out the pumpkin shapes and write a different locomotor task on each. For example, jump, walk backward, gallop, etc. Place the paper pumpkins at one end of the room and attach them to a long green paper vine using clothespins. Tell the children they are going to the pumpkin patch to pick a pumpkin. Have 2-3 children at a time get a pumpkin from the "patch" (they remove the paper pumpkin by squeezing the clothespin). Then have them perform the locomotor skill written on the pumpkin as they move back across the room to where they were sitting.

3. PROPRIOCEPTION

To help the children regroup after the vestibular task, have them sit in a circle and pass 2-3 real pumpkins, of various sizes, around the circle while seasonal music is playing. Discuss the weight of the pumpkins. Ask them "Which one is heaviest?"

4. BALANCE

Give the children one sheet of newspaper to crumble into a ball shape. Then have them walk on a balance beam while carrying the ball. At the end of the beam, they can throw the paper into the commercial jack-o-lantern trash bag. Repeat several times.

5. EYE-HAND COORDINATION

Use orange balloons for pretend pumpkins to volley back and forth to a partner. A jack-o-lantern face can be drawn on the balloon.

6. COOL-DOWN

Read a book about pumpkins. *Pumpkin Heads* by Wendell Minor (Scholastic, 2000) is one example. Discuss going to the pumpkin patch and picking out a pumpkin. Talk about how pumpkins are different sizes and shapes. Explain that some people like to carve pumpkins to make jack-o-lanterns and other people like to make and eat pumpkin pie.

7. FINE MOTOR

Have the children tear tissue paper into small pieces and glue onto a paper plate. Then have them glue a green stem on. Use milk jug lids to put the glue in, and a Q-tip to dip into the glue. This develops good prehension skills.

Materials

- (Optional: 5 orange felt pumpkins, 1 brown felt gate, flannel board)
- Using orange construction paper, copy 12 pumpkins of the reproducible pumpkin on page 177 and write a different locomotor task on each
- Long green bulletin board paper twisted into a "vine"
- Clothespins
- 2-3 real pumpkins
- CD/tape with seasonal music
- Balance beam
- Newspaper
- Commercial jack-o-lantern trash bags
- Orange balloons
- *Pumpkin Heads* by Wendell Minor (Scholastic, 2000)
- Small paper plates
- Orange tissue paper
- Pre-cut green stems
- Q-tips
- Glue
- Milk jug lids

THEME: RAIN

LESSON PLAN (QUICK VIEW)

1. **Warm-Up:** "Fun in the Rain" finger play and pretend "raining" on body parts
2. **Vestibular:** Rain water puddles to jump in
3. **Proprioception:** Theraband "walk in mud"
4. **Balance:** Follow the leader "Rain Dance" with shakers
5. **Eye-Hand Coordination:** Balloon volley clouds
6. **Cool-Down:** Book: *Rain Song* by Lezlie Evans
7. **Fine Motor:** Umbrella and rain picture

1. WARM-UP

Have the children say the following poem and perform the actions.
"Fun in the Rain"

> When the rain comes down,
> Drip, drop, drip, drop. (*Flutter fingers*)
> Windshield wipers
> Flip, flop, flip, flop. (*Move arms back and forth*)
> And boots in puddles,
> Plip, plop, plip, plop. (*Stomp feet*)
> I wish the rain would never stop.
> Drip, drop, drip, drop, (*Flutter fingers*)
> Flip, flop, flip, flop, (*Move arms back and forth*)
> Plip, plop, plip, plop, PLOP!
> (*Stomp feet, then stomp 2 feet at the same time on final "PLOP"*)

For the next warm-up activity, have the children "wake up their muscles" by wiggling their fingers like rain drops on top of each body part as you name the part. For example, "Wake up your arms" (the children wiggle their fingers while touching their arms, moving their hand up and down each arm). This may be repeated for legs, head, tummy, knees, elbows, shoulders, etc.

2. VESTIBULAR

Cut out approximately 15 blue construction paper "rain water puddles" and tape them to the floor in a circle. Explain to the children that when it rains, small water puddles form on the ground, and it is fun to jump into the puddles to make a big splash! Have the children each stand on a "water puddle" to start the activity. The children are going to jump with feet together onto the puddles around the circle. All the children can go at the same time, but monitor for safety as some children may jump faster than others. Play music for several minutes while the children are jumping. They can also stop and change direction.

3. PROPRIOCEPTION
Tie a 3-ft. piece of theraband together to form a circle. Make one for each child. Have the children put the theraband around their ankles and walk around the room pretending to be walking through "mud."

4. BALANCE
Tell the children that long ago, when the weather was very dry and the people needed rain, they would perform a "rain dance." Give each child a shaker (see below how to make a shaker) and ask them to follow the teacher leader as he/she performs a "rain dance." The teacher leader does a variety of balance tasks while shaking the shaker. Examples include: standing on one foot, then the other, standing heel to toe and balancing, hopping on one foot, then the other, jumping and turning around, etc.

5. EYE-HAND COORDINATION
Divide the children into partners. Give each set of partners an inflated white balloon. Tell them that the balloon is a pretend cloud and that they need to keep it in the sky for as long as they can. Have them count how many times they can hit the balloon without letting it touch the ground.

6. COOL-DOWN
Read a book about rain. One example is *Rain Song* by Lezlie Evans, illustrated by Cynthia Jabar (Scholastic, 1995). Talk about umbrellas, raincoats, and rain boots. Ask the children if they use those when it is raining. Discuss thunder and lightning, and help the children to understand that there is usually nothing to be afraid of when the thunder is booming.

7. FINE MOTOR
Copy the picture of the umbrella top on page 178 – 1 for each child. Have the children draw a handle for the umbrella. Using Q-tips for paintbrushes, have the children dip them into blue tempera paint and make dots of raindrops around the umbrella picture. Finally, have them sprinkle glitter on the wet paint.

Materials
- Approximately 15 blue construction paper "rain water puddles" (tape to floor in circle)
- Music tape or CD
- 3 ft. piece of theraband tied together to form a circle – 1 for each child
- Home-made shakers – 1 for each child (collect empty film containers or similar containers and fill partially with rice)
- White balloons – 1 for every pair of children
- *Rain Song* by Lezlie Evans, illustrated by Cynthia Jabar (Scholastic, 1995)
- Copies of umbrella picture on page 178 – 1 for each child
- Crayons or markers
- Q-tips
- Glitter
- Blue tempera paint poured into small flat containers

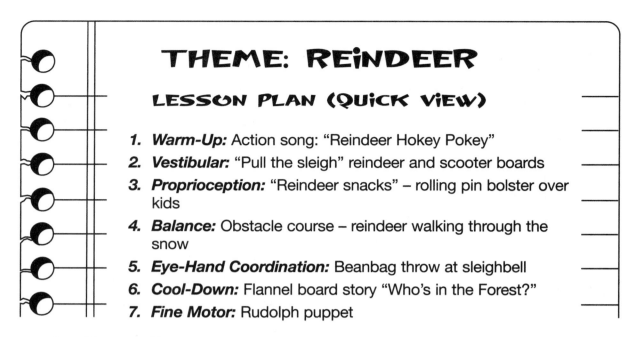

THEME: REINDEER

LESSON PLAN (QUICK VIEW)

1. **Warm-Up:** Action song: "Reindeer Hokey Pokey"
2. **Vestibular:** "Pull the sleigh" reindeer and scooter boards
3. **Proprioception:** "Reindeer snacks" – rolling pin bolster over kids
4. **Balance:** Obstacle course – reindeer walking through the snow
5. **Eye-Hand Coordination:** Beanbag throw at sleighbell
6. **Cool-Down:** Flannel board story "Who's in the Forest?"
7. **Fine Motor:** Rudolph puppet

1. WARM-UP

From *Great Big Holiday Celebrations* by Jean Warren (Warren Publishing House, 1991)
"Reindeer Hokey Pokey"
Sung to: "Hokey Pokey"
Perform actions along with the words.

> You put your antlers in, You put your antlers out, You put your antlers in,
> And shake them all about. You do the Reindeer Pokey and you turn yourself around.
> That's what it's all about.

> Additional Verses: "You put your front legs in; You put your hind legs in; You put
> your reindeer tail in; You put your reindeer body in."

2. VESTIBULAR

Have a child sit on a scooter board and hold onto the ends of a jump rope, while another child pulls him across the room, as if a reindeer were pulling santa in his sleigh. Optional: The children can wear reindeer antlers made from brown construction paper (copy reproducible antlers from page 179) and Santa hats. Switch partners to allow the children to experience both pulling and riding.

3. PROPRIOCEPTION

Explain to the children that the reindeer are hungry and need a cookie snack. Divide the class into groups with 2-3 children per group. While one child lies on his or her tummy, the other children roll a bolster on top of the child. (A rolling pin may be used if a bolster is not available.) Be sure to supervise the children for safety. Next, the children gently press cookie cutters on the child's back. Switch partners.

4. BALANCE

Place a long flat box filled with styrofoam peanuts in the middle of the room. Have the children line up and walk "like reindeer" through the "snow" to Santa's workshop. Play holiday music in the background. Children take turns stepping into the box, walking through the box, and stepping out of the box. Reinforce use of prepositions.

5. EYE-HAND COORDINATION

Explain to the children that Santa's reindeer wore bells so that they could be heard on Christmas Eve when flying to the children's houses. The children are going to throw a beanbag at a "sleighbell" and try to make it ring. Suspend 2-3 large bells from the ceiling. Have the child stand about 3-4 feet away and throw a beanbag to try to hit the bell. It is best to place a marker on the floor for the children to stand on. 2-3 children can go at the same time.

6. COOL-DOWN

An example flannel board story is "Who's in the Forest?" from *FlannelGraphs* by Jean Stangle (Fearon Teacher Aids, David S. Lake Publishers, 1986). Piece together the flannel pieces of the "reindeer" head as you read the story. Have the children recite the repeated phrase "They watched and watched and waited and waited."

7. FINE MOTOR

Adapted from *Great Big Holiday Celebrations* (Warren Publishing House, 1991).

Give each child a triangle drawn on brown construction paper. Have them trace the triangle and cut it out. Position the triangle with one point facing downward. Using Q-tips for dipping in the glue, the children glue 2 small brown triangle ears on top of the big triangle. Then they glue on 2 white circle eyes with small black circle pupils. They glue red glitter to a red circle nose, then glue it onto the bottom of the triangle. Finally, they tape on 2 small sticks for antlers. Reinforce shape identification while the children work.

Materials

- 2 scooter boards
- 2 jump ropes
- (Optional: 2 Santa hats, 2 brown construction paper reindeer antlers; see page 179 for pattern)
- Several bolsters and/or rolling pins
- Cookie cutters
- Long flat box filled with styrofoam peanuts
- Holiday music
- 2-3 large bells
- Beanbags
- Flannel board story "Who's in the Forest?" from *FlannelGraphs* by Jean Stangle (Fearon Teacher Aids, David S. Lake Publishers, 1986)
- Felt pieces for flannel board story (1 large brown triangle, 2 small brown triangles, 2 black rectangles for antlers, 2 white circles, 2 black circles, 1 red circle)
- Large triangle drawn on brown construction paper (make the outline wide for easier cutting) – 1 for each child
- Scissors
- Glue placed in milk jug lids
- Q-tips
- Pre-cut for each child – 2 small brown triangles, 2 white circles, 2 small black circles, 1 red circle
- Red glitter
- Small sticks – 2 for each child (reindeer antlers)

THEME: SCARECROWS

LESSON PLAN (QUICK VIEW)

1. **Warm-Up:** Book: *The Little Old Lady Who Was Not Afraid of Anything* by Linda Williams
2. **Vestibular:** Tunnel crawl with gloves and shirt shaking
3. **Proprioception:** Boot stomping and theraband stretch
4. **Balance:** Balance beam with hat
5. **Eye-Hand Coordination:** Crepe paper wind blowing/scaring the crows
6. **Cool-Down:** Action song: "Scarecrow"
7. **Fine Motor:** Stuffed paper bag scarecrow head

1. WARM-UP

Read the book *The Little Old Lady Who Was Not Afraid of Anything* by Linda Williams, illustrated by Megan Lloyd (HarperCollins Publishers, 1986). (The activities in this lesson plan relate directly to the story of the book.)

Directions: (Have the children remove shoes) Divide the classroom into 5 centers. Each of these centers imitates actions in the book. Form small groups for each center. The children will spend 5 minutes at each center and then rotate to the next center. Cue the children that it is time to rotate by turning the lights out briefly in the room. Continue until the children have all had turns at each center. Have the children perform the sensorimotor tasks described below.

2. VESTIBULAR

"Clap, clap" gloves center. Have each child put on a pair of gloves, clap their hands together, and repeat the words "clap, clap." They can crawl through the tunnel.

"Shake, shake" shirt center. Have each child put on an oversized shirt and practice buttoning. They can shake their arms to mimic the actions and repeat the words "shake, shake."

3. PROPRIOCEPTION

"Stomp, stomp" boot center. Place paper (copy reproducible corncobs on page 180) or real corncobs in a rectangle around the floor in a 3x6' area. Have the children put one adult-sized boot on either foot and pretend to stomp down the corn-row by walking around the area stomping the boot. The children can repeat the words in the book "stomp, stomp."

"Wiggle, wiggle" pants center. Show the children how to use a therapy exercise band by putting it under one foot and pulling it with both hands. Pretend these are pants and mimic the actions in the book. The children can repeat the words "wiggle, wiggle." Hula-hoops may be used as space markers.

4. BALANCE

"Nod, nod" hat center. Have the children walk on a balance beam wearing a hat. (At the end of the balance beam place a pumpkin or jack-o-lantern on a chair.) After children walk to the end of the balance beam, have them put the hat on the pumpkin head and repeat the words "nod, nod."

5. EYE-HAND COORDINATION

Give each child a piece of crepe paper about 1-2' long. Have them pretend to "scare" the crows away with the wind. The children create wind when they move the crepe paper streamer around. Play "Follow the Leader" and have the children imitate drawing shapes in the air (circle, square, triangle – pre-writing shapes), moving the crepe paper in all directions, such as up high, down low, behind, in front of, beside, etc.

6. COOL-DOWN

Have the children follow this action poem and repeat it several times.
From *Great Big Holiday Celebrations* by Jean Warren
(Warren Publishing House, 1991)

Scarecrow, scarecrow turn around.
Scarecrow, scarecrow touch the ground.
Scarecrow, scarecrow reach up high.
Scarecrow, scarecrow touch the sky.
Scarecrow, scarecrow bend down low.
Scarecrow, scarecrow touch your toe.
(Have the children put their shoes back on.)

7. FINE MOTOR

Give the children a paper bag each and have them draw a face on it. Then have them crumble newspaper up and stuff the paper sack with it. Twist and tape the bag closed. Let them glue on a pre-cut felt hat and small square "patches" of material. Then they glue raffia for hair. Finally, have them tie a pre-cut material triangle scarf around the "neck," which is the end of the bag that has been taped.

Materials

- *The Little Old Lady Who Was Not Afraid of Anything* by Linda Williams (HarperCollins Publishers, 1986)
- 3-5 pairs of child's size gloves
- 3-5 adult-size shirts, preferable plaid flannel
- Paper corn (copy from page 180) or real corncobs – enough to outline a 3x6' area
- 2 pairs of adult-size boots
- Therapy band, about 5 pieces 3' long
- (Optional: Hula-hoops)
- Tunnel
- Balance beam
- 2 hats
- Pumpkin or jack-o-lantern – real or plastic
- Crepe paper streamers, about 1-2' long – 1 for each child
- Small paper sacks, newspaper, glue, markers, tape, pre-cut triangle felt hats, pre-cut 1x1" material patches (use pinking shears for effect), pre-cut triangle shape scarf, raffia (may be purchased at craft store) – 1 for each child

THEME: SHAPES

LESSON PLAN (QUICK VIEW)

1. **Warm-Up:** Song from Hap Palmer's *Sally the Swinging Snake* – "Everything has a shape"
2. **Vestibular:** The Shape Shake game ("Hokey Pokey")
3. **Proprioception:** Square box push
4. **Balance:** Rope shape walk
5. **Eye-Hand Coordination:** Beanbag shapes catch/throw
6. **Cool-Down:** Book: *The Shape of Things* by Dayle Ann Dodds
7. **Fine Motor:** Shape picture

1. WARM-UP

Follow the directions in Hap Palmer's song "Everything has a shape" from *Sally the Swinging Snake.*

2. VESTIBULAR

"The Shape Shake" from *Early Years Thematic Notes: Shapes* by Marcia Gresko (Frank Schaffer Publications, 1993).

Give each child several different construction paper shapes to use for this activity (i.e., square, circle, triangle, diamond). Have the children stand in a circle and perform the "Hokey Pokey" game using the adapted version below.

> You put your circle in. You put your circle out.
> You put your circle in and shake it all about.
> You wave it up high, and you wave it down low.
> That's how the shape shake goes.

Finish song with the other shapes (square, triangle, rectangle).

3. PROPRIOCEPTION

Teach the children about boxes and squares. Have one child sit in a box and another push the box across the room and back again. Have 2 boxes at a time so that 4 children are taking turns. For children with low muscle tone or weakness who have difficulty pushing the box, place one large or two small scooter boards under the box.

4. BALANCE

Divide the children into partners. Design shapes on the floor using the jump ropes. Have the children walk on their jump rope shape. Change the rope to a different shape.

5. EYE-HAND COORDINATION

Have the children stay with their partners from the previous activity. Give them a beanbag to throw and catch. Let the children identify the shape of their beanbag. You may use different-shaped beanbags.

6. COOL-DOWN

Read a book about shapes. *The Shape of Things* by Dayle Ann Dodds (Scholastic, 1994) is one example. Ask the children to identify the different shapes in the book and objects that the shapes represent. Find shapes in the classroom, such as a rectangle door, a square block, or a circle globe.

7. FINE MOTOR

Give each child one large piece of construction paper (11x18"), and a pre-cut square, triangle, diamond, and circle. To save time, you can use the shapes from the "Hokey Pokey" game. Demonstrate creating a house by gluing the square and triangle on the construction paper, a kite by gluing the diamond on the top of the paper, and a sun by gluing the circle in the top corner of the paper. The children can draw grass on the bottom, a tail string for the kite, and lines around the sun.

Materials

- Hap Palmer's *Sally the Swinging Snake* – "Everything has a shape"
- Pre-cut shapes from construction paper (square, triangle, circle, diamond) – 1 for each child
- 2 large boxes
- Jump ropes – 1 per pair of children
- Beanbags of different shapes – 1 per pair of children
- *The Shape of Things* by Dayle Ann Dodds (Scholastic, 1994)
- Construction paper (11x18") – 1 for each child
- Crayons or markers
- Glue (put glue in milk jug lids and use Q-tips to glue with)

THEME: SPIDERS

LESSON PLAN (QUICK VIEW)

1. **Warm-Up:** Finger play and song: "The Itsy, Bitsy Spider"
2. **Vestibular:** Obstacle course spider web
3. **Proprioception:** Scooter board – crawling like a spider
4. **Balance:** Jump rope spider web
5. **Eye-Hand Coordination:** Ball of string throw/catch
6. **Cool-Down:** Book: *The Very Busy Spider* by Eric Carle
7. **Fine Motor:** Paper plate spider web

1. WARM-UP

Have the children sing the familiar song "The Itsy, Bitsy Spider" while performing the finger actions. Repeat several times.

> The itsy, bitsy spider went up the waterspout.
> Down came the rain and washed the spider out.
> Up came the sun, and dried up all the rain.
> And the itsy, bitsy spider went up the spout again.

2. VESTIBULAR

Create a large web by attaching crepe paper streamers to furniture. Have the children pretend to be a spider crawling through, over, under, and/or around their "web." At the end of the obstacle course, have them crawl through a tunnel pretending it is their cocoon. Repeat several times. (Be sure to show pictures of a spider web and cocoons prior to the activity to familiarize the children with the vocabulary.)

3. PROPRIOCEPTION

Have the children take turns pretending to crawl like a spider by lying prone* on a scooter board. They can use their arms and legs to propel themselves across the floor and back again. Have 2-3 scooter boards so that several children can take turns at the same time, but be sure to have plenty of space.

4. BALANCE

Place several jump ropes on the floor to form a spider web shape. Have the children walk on the spider web ropes. Show them how to walk on the rope heel to toe, sideways, or even backwards for an added challenge.

5. EYE-HAND COORDINATION

Have the entire group of children stand in a circle. The children toss a ball of string/yarn with one hand across the circle to a friend while holding the string with the other hand. By the time the ball of string goes around the circle, it will have created a spider web. To undo the web, have the children throw the ball of string back to the child who threw it to them. They have to wrap the string around the ball before they throw it back to the next child. (This may require adult assistance.)

6. COOL-DOWN
Read a book about spiders. One example is *The Very Busy Spider* by Eric Carle (Scholastic, 1984). Count how many legs spiders have, and discuss why they spin webs and what they eat.

7. FINE MOTOR
Cut several small slits around the edge of a paper plate about 1" apart. Have the children color the paper plate black. (Use the side of a crayon with the paper removed to develop finger strength.) Give each child a strand of white yarn and have them wrap the yarn around the paper plate, securing it in the slits around the edge. Leave a piece of the yarn dangling and attach a paper (see reproducible pattern on page 182) or plastic spider.

Materials
- Crepe paper (attach to furniture to create a web)
- Tunnel (8-ft. long tube of ribbed knit material)
- 2-3 scooter boards
- Jump ropes
- Ball of string/yarn
- *The Very Busy Spider* by Eric Carle (Scholastic, 1984)
- Paper plates with slits cut around the edge – 1 for each child
- Black crayons (remove paper on the outside edge)
- White yarn – 1 strand for each child
- Plastic or paper spider – 1 for each child (copy from page 181)

THEME: SPRING FLOWERS

LESSON PLAN (QUICK VIEW)

1. **Warm-Up:** Pretend seed growing into a flower
2. **Vestibular:** Obstacle course to plant a seed
3. **Proprioception:** Human plow
4. **Balance:** Balance beam – picking paper flowers
5. **Eye- Hand Coordination:** Seeds blowing – bubbles
6. **Cool-Down:** Book: *Planting a Rainbow* by Lois Ehlert
7. **Fine Motor:** Handprint flowers

1. WARM-UP

Have the children squat and pretend to be a seed getting ready to grow into a flower. As you say, "Now, here comes the rain and the sunshine," the children slowly get up and reach their arms toward the sky. Standing on tiptoes, they pretend to be a flower growing and blooming.

2. VESTIBULAR

Set up a circular obstacle course with objects to climb over, crawl under, crawl through, jump over, step on, etc. Give each child a real flower seed to hold. Have them move through the obstacle course several times. As they are finishing their last turn, have them plant their seed in a paper cup filled with soil. (Watch it grow over the next few weeks.)

3. PROPRIOCEPTION

Show the children a picture of a plow. Explain what a plow is and why it is used to dig the soil. Divide the children into partners. Using a mat, have each partner group take turns performing the human plow.* One child places his/her hands on the mat, while the other picks up the partner's feet and "walks" him/her down the mat. Switch partners and repeat. Be sure to match children with partners of equal size.

4. BALANCE

Set up a balance beam on the floor with paper (copy reproducible flower on page 182) or real flowers along both sides. (At least 2-3 flowers per child.) Have the children take turns walking across the balance beam and squatting to "pick a flower," recovering, and then taking the flower to put in a vase. Repeat several times.

5. EYE-HAND COORDINATION

Explain to the children that the wind blows flower seeds to a new "home" where the seeds fall to the ground and grow. Tell them that the bubbles are pretend flower seeds. Have the children stand in a circle. Blow bubbles and let the children pop the bubbles using their index finger.

6. COOL-DOWN

Read a book about springtime flowers. One example is *Planting a Rainbow* by Lois Ehlert (Voyager Books/Harcourt, 1988). Discuss how the sun and rain help a flower seed to grow. Talk about what different flowers look like. (Optional: Have real flowers as examples to pass around and smell.)

7. FINE MOTOR

Have the children cut a 6x2" piece of paper in half lengthwise. (You may need to draw a line for them). These will form 2 stems for the handprint flowers. Have the children glue the stems to an 8x10" piece of construction paper. They will then spread glue, using their index finger, along the entire bottom edge of the piece of construction paper. After they wipe off the glue, have them sprinkle real potting soil over the glue. Then they can glue fake plastic grass above the dirt to create a layered view. Finally, let them paint one of their hands with tempera paint and press it at the top of the each stem to create 2 flowers.

Materials

- Real flower seeds
- Paper cups with potting soil – 1 for each child with their names written on the cups
- Obstacle course equipment
- Mat
- Balance beam
- Paper or real flowers – 2-3 for each child; if paper, copy from page 182
- Vase
- Bubbles
- *Planting a Rainbow* by Lois Ehlert (Voyager Books/Harcourt, 1988)
- (Optional: Several real cut flowers)
- 6x2" piece of green construction paper with a line in the middle
- Scissors, glue, paintbrushes
- 8x10" piece of construction paper – 1 for each child
- Potting soil
- Fake grass
- Tempera paint
- Wet paper towels for wiping paint off hands

THEME: STONE SOUP

LESSON PLAN (QUICK VIEW)

1. **Warm-Up:** Story: *Stone Soup*
2. **Vestibular:** Rolling stones
3. **Proprioception:** Pass the "potato" (therapy ball)
4. **Balance:** Creek "stones" for walking on
5. **Eye-Hand Coordination:** Parachute w/plastic vegetables
6. **Cool-Down:** Song: "Making Stone Soup"
7. **Fine Motor:** Stone soup sponge paint picture

1. WARM-UP

Read the story about stone soup. There are a many different versions (e.g., *Stone Soup* by Jon Muth, Scholastic Inc., 2003; *Stone Soup* by Tony Ross, Fitzgerald, 2001).

2. VESTIBULAR

Have the children pretend to be stones. They each curl up into a "stone" and roll side to side. Be sure they have plenty of space between each other.

3. PROPRIOCEPTION

The children form a circle and assume a tall kneeling position.* Using a large therapy ball as a pretend giant potato, have the children pass it around the circle by pushing it with their hands. Continue for a few minutes, then have the children assume a supine flexion position.* Now the children can use their feet to kick the ball "potato."

4. BALANCE

Place several stepping stones on the floor. Tell the children that they have to cross the creek to get some small stones to make stone soup. Repeat walking across the stepping stones several times. On their last turn, let each child select a small stone to pretend to put in their "stone soup."

5. EYE-HAND COORDINATION

Have the children grasp a handle on a parachute. Place plastic vegetables in the center of the parachute. Tell the children they are going to make stone soup. The parachute is the pot, and they need to stir up the vegetables. Have them walk in a circle in one direction, then the other. Have them gently move the parachute up and down.

6. COOL-DOWN

From "Storytime Theme-saurus" compiled by Jean Warren (Warren Publishing House, 1989)
Song "Making Stone Soup"
Sung to: "The Paw Paw Patch"

Pick up a stone and put it in the pot.
Pick up a stone and put it in the pot.
Pick up a stone and put it in the pot.
Making stone soup together!

7. FINE MOTOR

Copy the reproducible kettle pot on page 183 for each child. Mix up red (tomato), yellow (onion), and brown (potato) tempera paints. Have the children use small sponges to dip into each color and create vegetables inside their "pot." Have them glue a small stone on the paper inside their "pot."

Materials

- Story about stone soup (*Stone Soup* by Jon Muth, Scholastic Inc., 2003; *Stone Soup* by Tony Ross, Fitzgerald, 2001)
- Large therapy ball
- Stepping stones
- Small rocks
- Parachute
- Plastic vegetables
- Reproducible kettle pot on page 183 – copy 1 for each child
- Red, yellow, brown tempera paint
- Sponges
- Small stones and glue

THEME: ST. PATRICK'S DAY
LESSON PLAN (QUICK VIEW)

1. **Warm-Up:** Book: *Hooray for St. Patrick's Day!* by Joan Holub
2. **Vestibular:** "Follow the Leader" – Irish dancing with green streamers
3. **Proprioception:** Pretend planting kid "potatoes"
4. **Balance:** Rainbow jumping
5. **Eye-Hand Coordination:** Shamrock fishing
6. **Cool-Down:** Passing hot/cold potatoes
7. **Fine Motor:** Shamrock necklace

1. WARM-UP
Read a book about St. Patrick's Day. *Hooray for St. Patrick's Day!* by Joan Holub, illustrated by Paul Meisel (Puffin Books, 2002), is one example. Ask if any of the children are Irish or know somebody who is. Discuss the events surrounding St. Patrick's Day, why people wear green, etc.

2. VESTIBULAR
Give each of the children a green crepe paper streamer. Play some Irish music and have the children follow the teacher leader, moving their streamers up and down, back and forth, around and around, and moving their bodies by marching, turning around, jumping, etc.

3. PROPRIOCEPTION
Explain to the children that they are going to pretend to plant potatoes because the Irish people love potatoes. Have each child take a turn pretending to be a "potato" by curling up into a ball with the back toward to ceiling. Place a beanbag chair (pretend dirt) over the child and have several other children gently push down. Repeat until all the children have had a turn to be "planted." Several children can take a turn at the same time, if you have several beanbag chairs.

4. BALANCE
Explain to the children that on St. Patrick's Day, rainbows are special because they can bring good luck. For this activity, have ready a 5x11" piece of construction paper in each of the rainbow colors (red, orange, yellow, green, blue, violet). Tape the red piece of construction paper to the floor. Have the children form a line and take turns jumping over the red paper. Then tape the orange piece of construction paper to the floor, right next to the red paper, and have them jump over both colors. Continue until all of the rainbow colors are taped adjacent to each other on the floor and the children have all had a turn to jump over them.

5. EYE-HAND COORDINATION

Cut out at least 12 shamrocks (copy reproducible pattern on page 184) and place a paperclip on each. Have the children stand in a circle and place the shamrocks on the floor in the middle of the circle. Using 2-3 hand-made magnet fishing poles, allow each child to take a turn "catching" a shamrock. Numbers, shapes or letters can be written on the shamrocks for the children to identify them as they "catch" the shamrock.

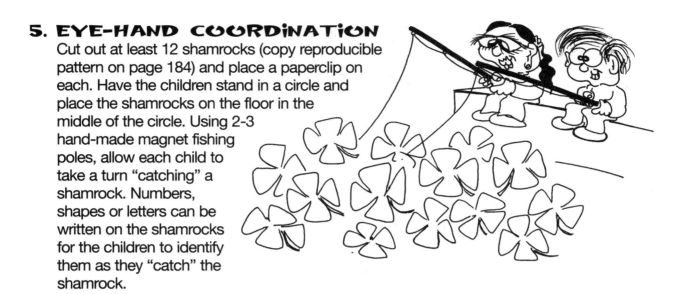

6. COOL-DOWN

Have ready one potato that has been warmed in the microwave (about 1 minute) and one potato that has been chilling in the refrigerator. Explain to the children that potatoes are symbolic of St. Patrick's Day because the Irish ate many potatoes. Have the children pass the hot/cold potatoes around in a circle. Ask them to feel the temperature of the potatoes and describe which one is hot and which one is cold.

7. FINE MOTOR

Have each child cut a straw into 1-inch pieces. Give them a pre-cut shamrock (see page 184) and have them spread glue on it and sprinkle it with green glitter. Punch a hole in the shamrock. Have the children lace the straw pieces and the shamrock onto yarn to create a necklace.

Materials

- 1 potato heated in the microwave – NOT TOO HOT!
- 1 potato cooled in the refrigerator
- Green crepe paper
- CD or tape with Irish music
- 1-2 beanbag chairs
- 5x11" piece of construction paper (1 each – red, orange, yellow, green, blue, violet)
- Paper shamrocks with paperclip attached – copy at least 1 for each child from page 184 (Optional: Write numbers, letters, shapes on the shamrocks)
- 2-3 hand-made fishing poles. Attach a string to a wooden dowel and tie a magnet to the end of the string.
- *Hooray for St. Patrick's Day!* by Joan Holub, illustrated by Paul Meisel (Puffin Books, 2002)
- Straws – 1 for each child
- Yarn with tape wrapped on one end for a "needle" and a piece of straw tied to the other end – 1 for each child
- Pre-cut shamrocks (page 184) – 1 for each child
- Scissors, glue, green glitter, hole punch

THEME: SUMMER FUN

LESSON PLAN (QUICK VIEW)
Note: These activities may be done outdoors.

1. **Warm-Up:** Suntan lotion rub and identification of body parts
2. **Vestibular:** Pretend swimming and toweling off
3. **Proprioception:** Sandbox "beach"
4. **Balance:** Balance board surfing
5. **Eye-Hand Coordination:** Beach ball volley
6. **Cool-Down:** Book: *Summer* by Alice Low
7. **Fine Motor:** Paper plate watermelons

1. WARM-UP
Give each child a small amount of suntan lotion and have them rub it on their arms, legs, feet, elbows, knees, cheeks, ears, nose, neck, etc. Ask them to identify each body part as they follow the teacher leader.

2. VESTIBULAR
As the children are waiting for their turn, let them pretend to sunbathe by lying down on their towels. Then let the children take turns and pretend to swim across a pool (mat) by moving on their tummy across the length of the mat and using their arms and legs to "swim." When they reach the end of the mat, let them towel off. Repeat several times.

3. PROPRIOCEPTION
Have the children pretend they are going to walk on a sandy beach. Place a large box filled with sand on the ground. (If done indoors, put a plastic drop cloth under the sandbox to keep the floor clean.) Have the children form a line and step into and out of the sandbox, digging their feet into the sand momentarily to feel the heavy weight of the sand. Repeat several times.

4. BALANCE
Using 2-3 balance boards, let the children pretend to be surfing on the water. Show the children pictures of people surfing so that they understand the concept. (Optional: Play the song "Surfing USA" by the Beach Boys.)

5. EYE-HAND COORDINATION
Divide the children into 2-3 groups and let them volley a beach ball back and forth to their friends.

6. COOL-DOWN

Read a book about summer. *Summer* by Alice Low, illustrated by Roy McKie (Beginner Books, A Division of Random House, 1991), is one example. Discuss fun summer activities the children enjoy, such as swimming, eating watermelon and hot-dogs, playing at a park, and building sand castles.

7. FINE MOTOR

Make paper plate watermelons. Have the children lie prone on their beach towels to complete the project. Have each child color their paper plate using the side of a crayon with the paper removed. Use a green crayon color on the outside edge of the plate and pink or red in the center. Have each child cut their paper plate in half to form 2 pieces of watermelon. Finally, have them glue several real watermelon seeds onto their paper plates.

Materials
- Suntan lotion (Note: Use non-allergenic lotion for children with skin sensitivity.)
- Mat
- Towels – 1 for each child (can bring from home)
- Box filled with sand (plastic drop cloth if done indoors)
- 2-3 balance boards (may be made from a 2x2' piece of wood with a wooden dowel hammered in the center)
- (Optional: Beach Boys' song "Surfing USA")
- 2-3 beach balls
- *Summer* by by Alice Low, illustrated by Roy McKie (Beginner Books, A Division of Random House, 1991)
- Paper plates with a line down the center to cut on – 1 for each child
- Real watermelon seeds
- Green and pink/red crayons with the paper removed
- Scissors, glue

THEME: THANKSGIVING/ NATIVE AMERICANS

LESSON PLAN (QUICK VIEW)

1. *Warm-Up:* Harvest game song
2. *Vestibular:* Scooter "canoes"
3. *Proprioception:* Pumpkin pie with mats
4. *Balance:* Obstacle course to plant Indian corn
5. *Eye-Hand Coordination:* Balloons with Indian symbols
6. *Cool-Down:* Book: *One Little, Two Little, Three Little Pilgrims* by B. G. Hennessy
7. *Fine Motor:* Indian headbands

1. WARM-UP

Place a basket with nuts and cranberries in the center of the circle of students. Have the children help count the cranberries and the nuts. Teach them the harvest song. Place one cranberry for each student around the room. While singing, have them each "bear walk"* to find a cranberry, place it in the basket, and sit down. Repeat.

"Harvest"
Sung to: "Ten Little Indians"
(From www.preschooleducation.com; original author unknown. Used with permission.)

Gather up the cranberries, Put them in the basket, Gather up the cranberries, Put them in the basket, Gather up the cranberries, Put them in the basket, It is Thanksgiving time.

Repeat with "Gather up the nuts." You can use paper, plastic, or real food as props.

2. VESTIBULAR

Show a picture of a canoe and talk about canoes and why Indians used them. Give each child a turn to sit on a scooter and pretend to row the "canoe" across the room and back. They can sit on the scooter and use their feet to propel for one turn, then sit on their knees and propel using their arms. Have 2-4 children go at the same time, depending on space.

3. PROPRIOCEPTION

Tell the children they are going to make a pretend pumpkin pie for Thanksgiving. Ask some of them to lie down on a mat. Then place another mat or a blanket on top of them. Have the other children gently press down on the mat pretending to squish the pumpkin to make a pie. Be sure they use open hands with straight arms when pressing down. Have the children switch places.

4. BALANCE
Create an obstacle course by placing a balance beam, stepping stones, and hula-hoops in a circle. Explain to the children that they are going to plant Indian corn and they have to cross a large river. Give each child a kernel of corn to carry with them. (You may use a picture of corn instead – see reproducible copy on page 180.) Show the children how to balance on the obstacle course equipment. Explain that they will plant the Indian corn seed in a cup of dirt after several times through the obstacle course. (Or place a paper picture of corn on the ground in a pretend "field.") Let the children repeat several times. Play Native-American music in the background.

5. EYE-HAND COORDINATION
Divide the children into partners and give them a balloon with Indian symbols drawn on it. Have them bat the balloon back and forth to a partner. They can practice math skills by counting how many times they hit the balloon without it touching the floor.

6. COOL-DOWN
Read a book about Thanksgiving. One example is *One Little, Two Little, Three Little Pilgrims* by B. G. Hennessy, illustrated by Lynne Cravath (Puffin Books, 1999). Have the children help count along with the story. Ask them "What is your favorite food to eat?" Ask them "What are you thankful for?," etc.

7. FINE MOTOR
Pre-cut strips of paper to fit around a child's head. Pre-cut 1-2 feather shapes (copy reproducible pattern on page 185) for each child. The children snip around the feather shapes to create ruffled edges. Have them draw Indian symbols on the strip of paper and practice writing the letters in their name as well. If a child is unable to form any letters, allow him to write a circle or plus shape. Staple the feather(s) to the strip of paper. Measure the strip to fit around the child's head and staple it closed.

Materials
- Basket
- Cranberries and nuts (real, plastic or paper) – 1 for each child
- 3-4 scooters
- 2 mats, or 1 mat and 1 blanket
- Balance beam, stepping stones, hula-hoops
- Indian corn
- CD or tape with Native-American music
- Balloons with Indian symbols drawn on them – 1 for two children to share
- *One Little, Two Little, Three Little Pilgrims* by B. G. Hennessy, illustrated by Lynne Cravath (Puffin Books, 1999)
- Strip of paper to fit around a child's head for a headband – 1 for each child
- Chalk, scissors, stapler
- Pre-cut paper feathers (page 185) – 1-2 per child

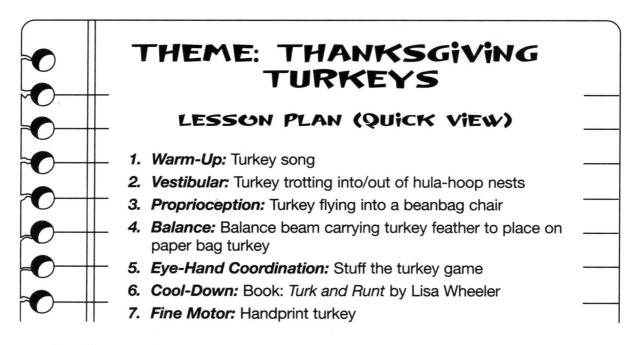

THEME: THANKSGIVING TURKEYS

LESSON PLAN (QUICK VIEW)

1. **Warm-Up:** Turkey song
2. **Vestibular:** Turkey trotting into/out of hula-hoop nests
3. **Proprioception:** Turkey flying into a beanbag chair
4. **Balance:** Balance beam carrying turkey feather to place on paper bag turkey
5. **Eye-Hand Coordination:** Stuff the turkey game
6. **Cool-Down:** Book: *Turk and Runt* by Lisa Wheeler
7. **Fine Motor:** Handprint turkey

1. WARM-UP

"Did You Ever See a Turkey?"
Sung to: "Did You Ever See a Lassie?"
(From www.preschooleducation.com; original author unknown. Used with permission.)

Did you ever see a turkey, a turkey, a turkey?
Did you ever see a turkey go this way and that?
Go this way and that way and this way and that way.
Did you ever see a turkey go this way and that?

2. VESTIBULAR

Show the children how to squat and flap their "wings." Place 3-4 hula-hoops on the floor. Explain that the hula-hoops are turkey nests and that the children have to walk into and out of the "nests" while moving around the room.

3. PROPRIOCEPTION

Divide the children into 2-3 groups with each group lining up next to a beanbag chair. Have the children take turns pretending to be a turkey, walking like turkeys* and flying into a "nest." Have them jump into the beanbag chair and gently press on their backs while they lie on the beanbag chair. Repeat several times.

4. BALANCE

(Prior to this activity, make a turkey out of a large paper bag by folding the edges down and taping on a construction paper turkey head, beak, and waddle.)

Have the children walk across a balance beam carrying a feather (real or paper – if paper, see reproducible copy on page 185). Play music in the background. After the last turn, help the children attach their feather to the paper bag turkey with tape.

130 Learn to Move, Move to Learn!

5. EYE-HAND COORDINATION

Place the large paper bag with feathers on it in the center of a circle of children. Have each child take turns crumbling newspaper and tossing it into the bag. Tell the children they are stuffing the turkey for Thanksgiving.

6. COOL-DOWN

Read a book about a turkey. One example is *Turk and Runt* by Lisa Wheeler, illustrated by Frank Ansley (Atheneum Books for Young Readers, 2002). Discuss why Runt always chased off the people who came to the farm. Talk about turkeys, where they are raised and what they like to eat.

7. FINE MOTOR

Have each child paint one hand using a paintbrush and make a handprint onto a piece of construction paper. Immediately wash the child's hand using a wet paper towel followed by a dry one. After washing hands, let them glue on a pre-cut orange triangle beak, a wiggle eye, and several small feathers.

Materials

- 3-4 hula-hoops
- 2-3 beanbag chairs
- Balance beam
- Feathers (real and/or paper) – 1 for each child; if paper, see page 185
- Music tape/CD
- Paper bag with construction paper turkey head
- Newspaper
- Book *Turk and Runt* by Lisa Wheeler, illustrated by Frank Ansley (Atheneum Books for Young Readers, 2002)
- Paper towels – 1 dry and 1 wet for each child
- Tempera paint and paintbrushes
- Large piece of construction paper
- Pre-cut orange construction paper triangles for beak – 1 for each child
- Wiggle eyes – 1 for each child

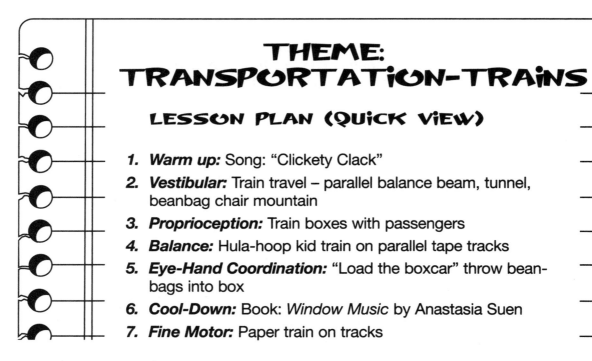

THEME: TRANSPORTATION-TRAINS

LESSON PLAN (QUICK VIEW)

1. **Warm up:** Song: "Clickety Clack"
2. **Vestibular:** Train travel – parallel balance beam, tunnel, beanbag chair mountain
3. **Proprioception:** Train boxes with passengers
4. **Balance:** Hula-hoop kid train on parallel tape tracks
5. **Eye-Hand Coordination:** "Load the boxcar" throw bean-bags into box
6. **Cool-Down:** Book: *Window Music* by Anastasia Suen
7. **Fine Motor:** Paper train on tracks

1. WARM-UP

Sung to: "Row, Row Your Boat"
(From www.preschooleducation.com; original author unknown. Used with permission.)

The children can make train motions while singing the song by moving their arms back and forth with elbows bent.

> Ride, ride, ride the train.
> Quickly down the track.
> Clickety, clickety, clickety, clack.
> When will you be back? (*Repeat several times*)

2. VESTIBULAR

Set up an obstacle course with 2 pieces of tape placed side by side for a "train track," a beanbag chair for a "mountain," and a tunnel. Have the children pretend they are going to travel on a train and have them move through the obstacle course several times.

3. PROPRIOCEPTION

Using two large boxes with "train wheels" drawn on the side, have one child pretend to be the passenger and sit in a box while a partner pushes the boxes across the room and back. Have the children trade places. Continue until every child has had a turn to both ride and push. Children with decreased strength can push a child "passenger" on a scooter board.

4. BALANCE

Have children create a human train by using small hula-hoops. Children hold a hula-hoop around their waist while standing in a line. Then they grasp onto the hula-hoop of the child standing in front of them. After all the children are hooked together, they move across pretend train tracks made from 2 equal-sized balance beams placed parallel on the floor.

5. EYE-HAND COORDINATION

Place the 2 boxes that were used for the proprioception activity on the floor about 5 feet from 2 place markers. Explain to the children that they are going to load the train "boxcar." Divide the children into 2 groups and have them take turns standing on the place markers tossing beanbags into the train "boxcar."

6. COOL-DOWN

Read a book about trains. One example is *Window Music* by Anastasia Suen, illustrated by Wade Zahares (Puffin Books, 1998). Discuss different types of trains, such as those that carry people (Amtrak) and those that carry cargo (coal). Have the children help count how many train cars are in the book. Ask them to name the shape of a train car.

7. FINE MOTOR

Copy the reproducible parallel train tracks on page 186, 1 for each child. Have the children draw vertical lines connecting the horizontal lines to represent railroad tracks. Then have the children cut out 1-3 rectangular-shaped "train cars" and glue them to the train tracks. Finally, have them draw circle wheels on the "train cars."

Materials

- 2 pieces of tape about 5' long placed on the floor parallel to each other
- Tunnel
- Beanbag chair
- 2 boxes big enough for a child to sit inside with wheels drawn on the side of the box
- (Optional: Scooter board for adaptation)
- Hula-hoops/rings – 1 for each child
- 2 balance beams (low to the ground – 2x4' boards may be used) placed side by side
- 6 small beanbags and 2 place markers
- *Window Music* by Anastasia Suen, illustrated by Wade Zahares (Puffin Books, 1998)
- Copy the reproducible parallel train tracks on page 186 – 1 for each child
- Rectangle shapes drawn on construction paper for each child to cut out – 1-3 for each child
- Scissors, glue, markers

THEME: VALENTiNE'S DAY

LESSON PLAN (QUiCK ViEW)

1. **Warm-Up:** "Sweetheart Dance" action song
2. **Vestibular:** Locomotor heart exercises
3. **Proprioception:** "Post office" Valentine delivery on scooter-board
4. **Balance:** "Cupid Says" balance game
5. **Eye-Hand Coordination:** Heart-shape balloon volley
6. **Cool-Down:** Book *Valentine Mice* by Bethany Roberts
7. **Fine Motor:** Coffee filter hearts/eyedropper painting

1. WARM-UP

Cut small heart shapes from the reproducible pattern on page 187 out of red, yellow and blue construction paper. Give each child one heart and have them stand in a circle. Sing the song below and have the children follow the directions.

"Sweetheart Dance"
(From www.preschooleducation.com; original author unknown. Used with permission.)
Sung to: "Skip to My Lou"

> Red hearts, red hearts, take a bow
> Yellow hearts, yellow hearts, take a bow
> Blue hearts, blue hearts, take a bow
> Now all hearts jump up right now.
> Yellow hearts, yellow hearts touch the ground
> Blue hearts, blue hearts touch the ground
> Red hearts, red hearts touch the ground
> Now all hearts turn round and round.
> Blue hearts, blue hearts, wit right down
> Red hearts, red hearts, sit right down
> Yellow hearts, yellow hearts sit right down.

2. VESTiBULAR

Cut out red paper hearts (make several copies of reproducible large heart on page 187) and write different locomotor tasks on each. For example, jump up and down, bear walk, jog in place, walk on tiptoes, march in place, gallop. Have the children stand in a circle and put the paper hearts in the center. Allow one child at a time to choose a heart. Have all of the children perform the locomotor tasks written on the heart selected.

3. PROPRIOCEPTION

Place a pretend mailbox at one end of the room. Have one child sit on a scooter board while another child pushes him/her to the "post office" to deliver a Valentine card. Two scooters can be used at one time if there is space. Have the children switch places. Repeat until all the children have had turns pushing and being pushed.

4. BALANCE

Have each child stand near a paper heart (use the small paper heart from the warm-up activity) that is taped to the floor. Acting as "Cupid," instruct the children to perform different balance tasks using prepositions. For example, "Cupid Says ("Simon Says") stand on one foot ON the heart, hop on one foot OVER the heart, jump backward OVER the heart, jump sideways BESIDE the heart, stand on tiptoes in FRONT of the heart, walk backwards AROUND the heart," etc.

5. EYE-HAND COORDINATION

Blow up 3-4 balloons and draw hearts on them with a permanent marker. Divide the children into 3-4 groups and have them practice volleying the balloon to each other.

6. COOL-DOWN

Read a book about Valentine's Day. One example is *Valentine Mice* by Bethany Roberts (Clarion Books, 2001). Talk about the shape and color of a heart. Discuss why people like to give Valentines to friends and loved ones.

7. FINE MOTOR

Fold a coffee filter in half and draw half of a heart shape on the fold. Prepare one for each child. Have the children cut along the line and then unfold the coffee filter to reveal a heart. (Have an adult write the child's first name in permanent marker on their heart.) Have them use an eye-dropper and squeeze red food colored water onto the heart. Let dry, then hang it in the window for a "stained glass" look.

Materials
- Small red, yellow, and blue paper hearts (for Warm-Up) (see page 187)
- Large red paper hearts with locomotor tasks written on each (see page 187)
- 2 scooter boards
- Valentine's cards – at least 1 for each child
- 3-4 balloons
- *Valentine Mice* by Bethany Roberts (Clarion Books, 2001)
- Coffee filters folded in half with half a heart shape drawn on fold
- Red food coloring mixed with water
- Eye-droppers

THEME: WEATHER/WIND

LESSON PLAN (QUICK VIEW)

1. **Warm-Up:** Pretend wind of crepe paper streamers
2. **Vestibular:** Spinning kid tornadoes
3. **Proprioception:** Parachute with heavy pillow clouds
4. **Balance:** Pretend tree with fan "wind"
5. **Eye-Hand Coordination:** White balloon clouds toss/catch
6. **Cool-Down:** Book: *The Wind Blew* by Pat Hutchins
7. **Fine Motor:** Paper kites

1. WARM-UP

Give each of the children a crepe paper streamer and have them pretend it is the wind. The children follow the teacher leader, moving the streamers using prepositional phrases (up/down, front/back, low/high) and pre-writing skills (draw a circle, plus, square in the air).

2. VESTIBULAR

Teach the children that the wind can blow strong and twisting. Then show them a picture of a tornado. (You may also want to talk briefly about tornado shelters, tornado drills.) Have the children pretend to be tornadoes by twirling around 2-3 times while standing, and then stop, rest, and twirl around in the other direction. Repeat only 1 time. (*Caution: Children with seizure disorders should not spin as it may induce a seizure. They can turn front/back slowly instead. Also, an occupational therapist must closely monitor any children with sensory integration difficulties to be sure they do not get too much vestibular input from this activity.*)

3. PROPRIOCEPTION

Have all the children stand in a circle and hold a handle of the parachute. Place heavy pillows in the center to represent clouds in the sky. The children follow directions given by the teacher leader and move the parachute up/down, slow/fast, etc., so that the "clouds" can float into the sky.

4. BALANCE

The children pretend to be trees blowing in the wind. They balance on one foot, then the other, while a fan is blowing on them. The trick is not to "Let the wind blow you down!"

5. EYE-HAND COORDINATION

Divide the children into 2-3 groups and have them toss and catch white balloon "clouds." Count how many times they can do this without the balloon touching the floor.

6. COOL-DOWN

Read a book about wind and weather. One example is *The Wind Blew* by Pat Hutchins (Scholastic, 1974). Have the children identify each object that the wind blows in the book. Ask the children how it feels to have the wind blow on their face, and if they have seen the wind blow tree leaves, a piece of paper or a flag, etc.

7. FINE MOTOR

Copy the reproducible kite shape on page 188 onto an 8x10" piece of paper, 1 for each child. Have the children trace the diamond shape with a marker or crayon and glue small pieces of cut-up wallpaper samples onto the "kite" diamond to create a collage. Finally, have them trace the curved line with glue and put a piece of yarn on top.

Materials

- Crepe paper cut into 1-2' pieces – 1 for each child
- Picture of a tornado
- Parachute
- 2-3 heavy pillows
- Electric fan
- 2-3 white balloons
- *The Wind Blew* by Pat Hutchins (Scholastic, 1974)
- Copy the reproducible kite shape on page 188 onto an 8x10" piece of paper – 1 for each child
- Yarn strings cut to size of curved line – 1 for each child
- Small cut-up pieces of wall paper samples
- Glue, crayons, markers

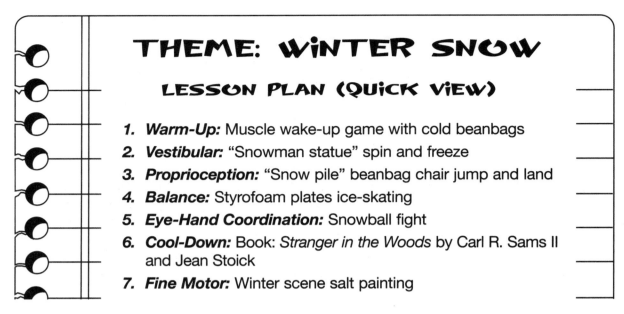

THEME: WINTER SNOW

LESSON PLAN (QUICK VIEW)

1. **Warm-Up:** Muscle wake-up game with cold beanbags
2. **Vestibular:** "Snowman statue" spin and freeze
3. **Proprioception:** "Snow pile" beanbag chair jump and land
4. **Balance:** Styrofoam plates ice-skating
5. **Eye-Hand Coordination:** Snowball fight
6. **Cool-Down:** Book: *Stranger in the Woods* by Carl R. Sams II and Jean Stoick
7. **Fine Motor:** Winter scene salt painting

1. WARM-UP

Give each child a cold beanbag. (Place beanbags in refrigerator ahead of time.) Instruct the children to wake up their muscles by rubbing the beanbag on different body parts. Say "Wake up your …" and demonstrate by rubbing the beanbag on arms, legs, neck, elbows, knees, hands, wrists, etc. The children will learn body part identification while receiving tactile input through temperature and deep-pressure touch.

2. VESTIBULAR

While the children are standing in a circle an arm's length from each other, have them spin around in a circle in one direction, then "freeze" on command, just like a snowman statue. Repeat in the other direction. Do this activity no more than twice in each direction. Watch children for overstimulation or complaints of headaches/tummy aches and have them discontinue the activity if necessary.

3. PROPRIOCEPTION

Place 1-3 large beanbag chairs around the room and divide the children into equal-sized groups. Demonstrate jumping into the "snow pile" and landing on knees, curling into a snowball, and finally crawling out. Have the children take turns performing this activity for several turns. Packing peanuts may be sprinkled onto the beanbag chairs for pretend "snow."

4. BALANCE

Give each child two styrofoam plates or cleaned meat trays. With their shoes off, have them use the styrofoam plates as ice skates by standing on them and pushing their legs, moving around the room maintaining balance. Music may be playing in the background for several minutes.

5. EYE-HAND COORDINATION

Divide the children into 2 equal groups and place one "team" on either side of a pretend snow wall. (This can be a mat propped up on the side.) Have the children assume a tall kneeling-on-knees position.* Give each child some newspapers to crumble into snowballs. After they have made their snowballs, say "ready, set, go!" and have them begin throwing the snowballs over the mat to the other team. Be sure to instruct safety and tell the children to throw the snowballs down low so that the children's eyes are protected.

6. COOL-DOWN

Read a book about winter snow. *Stranger in the Woods* by Carl R. Sams II and Jean Stoick (Carl R. Sams II Photography, 2000) is one suggestion. Talk about the color of snow, whether snow is cold or warm, and what causes snow to melt. Ask the children if they have ever made a real snow angel or snowman.

7. FINE MOTOR

Have the children cut out 2 green triangles for evergreen trees and glue them onto a piece of large blue construction paper. Have 3 white construction paper circles pre-cut (small, medium, and large sizes) for each child to glue to the paper scene and make a snowman. They can draw a face, arms, and buttons on the snowman. Finally, have them paint "snow" with white tempera paint mixed with salt.

Materials

- Beanbags
- Beanbag chairs sprinkles with packing peanuts
- Styrofoam plates or meat trays – 2 for each child
- Newspapers torn in half
- Mat or large cardboard box for a snow fort
- *Stranger in the Woods* by Carl R. Sams II and Jean Stoick (Carl R. Sams II Photography, 2000)
- Large blue construction paper – 1 sheet for each child
- Green triangles for cutting out – 2 for each child
- Pre-cut 3 white construction paper circles for each child (small, medium, large sizes)
- White tempera paint mixed with salt
- Paintbrushes, markers
- Music CD/tape

THEME: ZOO

LESSON PLAN (QUICK VIEW)

1. **Warm-Up:** Book: *At the Zoo* by Susan Canizares
2. **Vestibular:** Kangaroo ball hop
3. **Proprioception:** Elephant walk with ankle weights
4. **Balance:** "Monkey See, Monkey Do"
5. **Eye-Hand Coordination:** Feed the elephant – peanut toss
6. **Cool-Down:** Action song: "Monkey Arm Swing"
7. **Fine Motor:** Animal pictures with meat tray laced cage

1. WARM-UP

Read a book about the zoo. One example is *At the Zoo* by Susan Canizares (Scholastic Inc., 2000). Discuss the different animals that live at the zoo. Ask the children if they have ever visited a zoo.

2. VESTIBULAR

Have the children pretend to be kangaroos at the zoo. Let 2-3 children take turns at the same time. They hold a playground-size ball between their knees (using no hands) and hop across the room and back again. Allow all the children to take several turns.

3. PROPRIOCEPTION

Have children do elephant walking.* Place ankle weights on several children. Have all the children pretend to be elephants and walk around in a circle by clasping their hands together and swinging them back and forth. The children who are not wearing the ankle weights can stomp their feet while walking. Let all the children have a turn wearing the ankle weights. Play rhythmical music in the background. (Optional: Place shelled peanuts on the floor and have the children crush them by stomping on them.)

4. BALANCE

Cut out yellow construction paper to designate banana peels and tape them to the floor – 1 in front of each child. Tell the children that they are going to play a game called "Monkey See, Monkey Do." Explain that they need to follow the actions of the teacher leader. Using only non-verbal cues, have the children imitate you: balance on one foot, then the other on the banana peel; hop forward, then backward over the banana peel; squat on the banana peel; jump sideways over the banana peel; etc.

5. EYE-HAND COORDINATION
Have the children stand in a circle with a bucket in the center. Tape an elephant face to the bucket. Give each child several peanuts in the shell. Let them toss the peanuts, one at a time, into the bucket to feed the elephant.

6. COOL-DOWN
While the children are standing in the circle, have them hold hands. Teach them the following poem and have them swing their arms up and down together.

"Monkey Arm Swing"
(From www.preschooleducation.com; original author unknown. Used with permission.)

Little monkeys swinging in the tree,
All hold hands and swing with me.
Swing up high and swing down low,
Swing in the tree, now don't let go!
Swing, swing, like I do.
Swing like monkeys in the zoo.

7. FINE MOTOR
Let the children cut out pictures of zoo animals from magazines. Have them glue the animal pictures to a meat tray. (Prepare ahead of time by cutting small slits around the top and bottom of the meat tray.) Give each child a piece of string to wrap around the meat tray to create bars on a cage.

Materials
- Book *At the Zoo* by Susan Canizares (Scholastic Inc., 2000)
- 2-3 playground-size balls
- Ankle weights
- Music
- Yellow construction paper banana peels – 1 for each child
- Bucket with paper elephant face
- Peanuts in the shell
- Magazines
- Scissors, glue
- Meat trays – 1 for each child (cut small slits on top and bottom of meat tray)
- Yarn or string cut to size for meat tray bar cage – 1 for each child

BIBLIOGRAPHY AND SUGGESTED READINGS

The following sources provide additional background information about sensory integration, as well as ideas for sensorimotor activities that may be used when creating your own lesson plans. Ideas from some of the sources were also used in creating the lesson plans presented in this book.

Ayres, A. J. (1979). *Sensory integration and the child*. Los Angeles, CA: Western Psychological Services.

Beninghof, A. (1998). *SenseAble strategies: Including diverse learners through multisensory strategies.* Longmont, CO: Sopris West.

Bittinger, G. (1997). *Multisensory theme-a-saurus: Learning through the five senses.* Everett, WA: Totline Publications.

Bryte, K. (1996). *Classroom intervention for the school-based therapist: An integrated model.* San Antonio, TX: Therapy Skill Builders.

Bundy, A., Lane, S., & Murray, E. (2002). *Sensory integration theory and practice* (2nd ed.). Philadelphia, PA: F. A. Davis Company.

Clark, G., Frolek, & Ward S. (n.d.). *Sensory diet: Alerting the brain for learning (A guide for parents and teachers).* Johnston, IA: Heartland Area Education Division, Special Education Division.

Crawford, J., Hanson, J., Gums, M., & Neys, P. (1994). *Please teach all of me: Multisensory activities for preschoolers*. Longmont, CO: Sopris West.

Degangi, G. (1994). *Documenting sensorimotor progress: A pediatric therapist's guide*. San Antonio, TX: Therapy Skill Builders.

Degangi, G. (2000). *Pediatric disorders of regulation in affect and behavior: A therapist's guide to assessment and treatment.* San Diego, CA: Academic Press.

Duran, G., & Klenke-Ormiston, S. (1994). *Multi-play: Sensory activities for school readiness.* San Antonio, TX: Therapy Skill Builders.

Frick, S., Frick, R., Oetter, P., & Richter, E. (1996). *Out of the mouths of babes.* Hugo, MN: PDP Press.

Fuge, G., & Berry, R. (2004). *Pathways to play! Combining sensory integration and integrated play groups – Theme-based activities for children with autism spectrum and other sensory-processing disorders*. Shawnee Mission, KS: Autism Asperger Publishing Company.

Ganz, J. (1998). *Including SI: A guide to using sensory integration concepts in the school environment.* Bohemia, NY: Kapable Kids.

Gresko, M. (1993). *Early years thematic notes: Shapes.* Torrance, CA: Frank Shaffer Publications.

Haldy, M., & Haack, L. (1995). *Making it easy: Sensorimotor activities at home and school.* San Antonio, TX: Therapy Skill Builders.

Henry, D. (1998). *Tool chest for teachers, parents and students: A handbook to facilitate self-regulation.* Youngtown, AZ: Henry Occupational Therapy Services, Inc.

Inamura, K. (1998). *SI for early intervention: A team approach.* San Antonio, TX: Therapy Skill Builders.

Kane, K., & Anderson, M. (1998). *PT activities for pediatric groups.* San Antonio, TX: Therapy Skills Builders.

Kasser, S. L. (1995). *Inclusive games: Movement fun for everyone.* Champaign, IL: Human Kinetics.

Knickerbocker, B. M. (1980). *A holistic approach to learning disabilities.* Thorofare, NJ: C. B. Slack.

Korsten, J. B., & Dunn, D. K. (1989, 1993). *Every move counts.* Tucson, AZ: Responsive Management, Inc./Published by Therapy Skill Builders, a division of Communication Skill Builders, Inc.

Kranowitz, C. (1998). *The out of sync child: Recognizing and coping with sensory integration dysfunction.* New York: Skylight Press.

Myles, B., Cook, K., Miller, N., Rinner, L., & Robbins, L. (2002). *Asperger syndrome and sensory issues: Practical solutions for making sense of the world.* Overland Park, KS: Autism Asperger Publishing Company.

Scheerer, C. (1997). *Sensorimotor groups: Activities for school and home.* San Antonio, TX: Therapy Skill Builders.

Sheda, C. H., & Ralston, P. R. (1997). *Sensorimotor processing activity plans.* San Antonio, TX: Therapy Skill Builders.

Stangle, J. (1986). *Flannelgraphs.* Belmont, CA: Fearon Teacher Aids, David S. Lake Publishers.

Warren, J. (1991). *Great big holiday celebrations.* Everett, WA: Warren Publishing House.

Warren, J. (1991). *Storytime them-a-saurus.* Everett, WA: Warren Publishing House.

Wilbarger, P., & Wilbarger, J. L. (1991). *Sensory defensiveness in children aged 2-12. An intervention guide for parents and other caretakers.* Denver, CO: Avanti Educational Programs.

Williams, M. S., & Shellenberger, S. (1994). *How does your engine run? A leader's guide to the alert program for self regulation.* Albuquerque, NM: Therapy Works, Inc.

Williamson, G. G., & Anzalone, M. E. (2001). *Sensory Integration and self-regulation in infants and toddlers: Helping very young children interact with their environments.* Washington, DC: Zero to Three.

Wolfberg, P. J. (2003). *Peer play and the autism spectrum: The art of guiding children's socialization and imagination.* Shawnee Mission, KS: Autism Asperger Publishing Company.

RESOURCES

The following is a list of companies that provide large equipment, small supplies, and books that may be purchased for group activities.

Communication Skill Builders, 555 Academic Court, San Antonio, TX 78204-2498. 1-800-211-8378.

KAPLAN, P.O. Box 609, 1310 Lewisville-Clemmons Rd., Lewisville, NC 27023-0609; 1-800-334-2014.

Oriental Trading Company, Inc., P.O. Box 2308, Omaha, NE 68103-2308; 1-800-228-2269.

O.T. Ideas, Inc., 124 Morris Turnpike, Randolph, NJ 07869; (973) 895-3622.

PDP Products, 14398 North 59th St., Oak Park Heights, MN 55082; (651) 439-8865.

Pro-Ed, Inc., 8700 Shoal Creek Blvd., Austin, TX 78757-6897; 1-800-897-3202.

Sammons Preston, An AbilityOne Company, P.O. Box 5071, Bolingbrook, IL 60440-5071; 1-800-323-5547.

Sensory Integration International, P.O. Box 9012, Torrance, CA 90508; (310) 533-8338.

Southpaw Enterprises, Inc., 800 West Third St., Dayton, OH 45407-2805; 1-800-228-1698.

Therapy Skill Builders, 3830 E. Bellevue, Tucson, AZ 85733; (602) 323-7500.

Therapro, 225 Arlington St., Framingham, MA 01702-8723; 1-800-257-5376.

Western Psychological Services (WPS), 12031 Wilshire Blvd., Los Angeles, CA 90025; 1-800-222-2670.

WEBSITES

www.asperger.net Autism Asperger Publishing Company: An excellent website for locating a wide variety of resources to learn more about helping children with sensory processing problems.

www.childfun.com Childfun Family Website: Great resource for fun activity theme ideas you can use when creating your own lesson plans.

www.janbrett.com Jan Brett: This website offers free downloads and project ideas that coordinate with each of Jan Brett's books.

www.jewelcartoons.com Jewel Cartoons: At this site, you can find children's books that teach lessons about disability and diversity by the illustrator for *Learn to Move, Move to Learn!*

www.preschooleducation.com Preschool Education Discover the Fun in Learning: Wonderful resource for theme-based songs and music, games, snacks, book suggestions and free downloads for hours of creative enjoyment.

APPENDIX

Signs and Symptoms of Sensory Integration/Processing Dysfunction

Tactile
- [ ] Dislikes standing in line
- [ ] Bothered by tags on shirts
- [ ] Dislikes playing with messy things
- [ ] Reacts aversively to textured foods
- [ ] Likes only highly textured foods
- [ ] Does not react to falls, scrapes or bumps
- [ ] Touches everything walks touching the wall
- [ ] Constantly puts things in mouth

Proprioceptive
- [ ] Stamps feet or bangs with hands
- [ ] Writes or holds pencil too hard (or too soft)
- [ ] Plays too roughly
- [ ] Seems unaware of body in space – clumsy
- [ ] Handles toys roughly – lots of banging and breaking
- [ ] Deliberately falls or tumbles a lot
- [ ] Chews hard on things
- [ ] Demonstrates poor motor planning in gross-/fine-motor skills

Vestibular
- [ ] Wiggles around during seated activities
- [ ] Craves spinning or swinging
- [ ] Rocks while seated or standing
- [ ] Likes being upside down
- [ ] Is Constantly in motion
- [ ] Is afraid of movement
- [ ] Experiences car sickness
- [ ] Avoids playground equipment
- [ ] Fears having head tilted backward (e.g., hair washing)
- [ ] Is afraid to sit on a toilet

Auditory
- [ ] Covers ears or screams with sudden loud noises (e.g., vacuum cleaner, toilet flushing)
- [ ] Has difficulty locating sound
- [ ] Enjoys constantly making sounds (e.g., humming)
- [ ] Is constantly distracted by background sounds (e.g., fluorescent lights humming)
- [ ] Prefers music very loud

Vision
- [ ] Demonstrates poor eye contact
- [ ] Turns head to the side when looking at things
- [ ] Holds head very close to work
- [ ] Loses place on page when reading
- [ ] Has difficulty copying from the board
- [ ] Uses hand as a "visor" in bright sunlight or fluorescent lighting
- [ ] Has difficulty tracking a ball to catch

Arousal and Attending
- [ ] Is hyperactive and difficult to calm
- [ ] Has difficulty modulating emotional response
- [ ] Startles easily
- [ ] Is difficult to arouse and does not react to loud sounds, bright lights, etc.
- [ ] Has difficulty completing tasks
- [ ] Has difficulty transitioning from one task to another

Social Consciousness
- [ ] Reacts with laughter when someone expresses anger, sadness, fear
- [ ] Becomes fearful in social situations
- [ ] Does not spontaneously interact in a group
- [ ] Appears to be unaware of others' feelings
- [ ] Unable to identify happy/sad/angry faces

Olfactory/Gustatory
- [ ] Complains of things "smelling bad"
- [ ] Notices how people smell
- [ ] Reacts violently to smells
- [ ] Smells objects constantly
- [ ] Prefers foods that are highly spiced or totally bland
- [ ] Chooses very limited repertoire of foods (e.g., prefers smooth vs. texture)

From Brack, J. C. (2004). *Learn to Move, Move to Learn!* Shawnee Mission, KS: Autism Asperger Publishing Company. Copied with permission.

Progress Data Collection Form

Child: _____

Quarterly Date

Goals	First Quarter	Second Quarter	Third Quarter	Fourth Quarter
1)				
2)				
3)				
4)				
5)				
6)				
7)				
8)				
9)				
10)				
11)				
12)				
13)				
14)				
15)				
16)				
17)				
18)				
19)				
20)				

Progress Data Collection Form

Skill: _____

Children	Date	Met	Date	Met	Date	Met	Date	Met	Date	Met	Date	Met	Date	Met
1)														
2)														
3)														
4)														
5)														
6)														
7)														
8)														
9)														
10)														
11)														
12)														
13)														
14)														
15)														
16)														
17)														
18)														
19)														
20)														

Lesson Plans

Theme:_____

Lesson Plan (Quick View)

1. Warm-Up: _____
2. Vestibular: _____
3. Proprioception: _____
4. Balance: _____
5. Eye-Hand Coordination: _____
6. Cool-Down: _____
7. Fine Motor: _____

Details/Notes

Materials

☐ _____
☐ _____
☐ _____
☐ _____
☐ _____
☐ _____
☐ _____
☐ _____
☐ _____

Who's Responsible?

_____
_____
_____
_____
_____
_____
_____
_____

DEFINITIONS OF POSITIONS MENTIONED IN LESSONS

Bear Walk: Place hands and feet on the floor with belly side down. Walk on hands and feet forward with legs and arms straight and rear in the air. Do not let the knees touch the ground.

Caterpillar Crawl: This is a group task. Have the children all form a row and then assume a hands-and-knees position. The children grasp the ankles of the child in front of them forming a caterpillar chain, and move around the room as a whole group.

Crab Walk: Place hands and feet on the floor with belly side up. Move forward or backward using arms and legs.

Dog Crawl: Assume a hands-and-knees position. Shake head from side to side as if to shake water off "dog" ears.

Duck Walk: Assume a squatting position with arms bent so that the hands are under the armpits. Move around the room flapping arms while maintaining the squatting position.

Elephant Walk: While walking and stomping feet, clasp hands together and swing them back and forth hanging down low like an elephant's trunk.

Frog Squat and Hop: Assume a squat position with hands touching the floor. Begin to hop forward by springing up and down, each time touching the floor with both hands.

Gallop: While standing, keep one foot in front of the other and move around the room in a half-skip pattern.

Hands-and-Feet Position: Place hands and feet on the floor with rear in the air. Hold this position while stretching up onto toes.

Knee Walk: Assume tall kneeling position (see at right) and walk around the room in this position.

Log Roll: Lie down on a mat with arms either touching top of the head or straight down the side of the body. Roll first in one direction and then the other.

Prone Extension: Assume an "airplane" position. Belly is on the floor. The head, arms and legs are lifted off the floor. Be sure to keep the arms and legs straight.

Supine Flexion: Assume a "sit-up" position and hold it. Chin is tucked, legs are pulled to chest, and arms are folded across chest.

Tall Kneel: Kneel on the floor, hips in a straight alignment with body so that arms are free to use.

Tree Balance Yoga Pose: While standing, bring one foot up to touch the inside of the knee on the opposite leg. Hold this position as long as possible, while reaching arms up high. Repeat on the other leg.

Turkey Trot: Assume a squatting position with arms bent so that the hands are touching under the armpits. Move around the room flapping arms while maintaining the squatting position.

Wheelbarrow Walk/Plow: This requires 2 children. Child #1 places hands on the floor, and child #2 stands up and holds child #1's ankles. They move across a mat coordinated together. Child #2 walks on feet and continues to hold child #1's ankles, while child #1 uses arms to "walk," keeping elbows straight.

RECOMMENDED CHILDREN'S BOOKS

Are You My Mother?, P. D. Eastman (Random House, 1960)

At the Zoo, Susan Canizares (Scholastic, 2000)

Bear Snores On, Karma Wilson & Jane Chapman (Margaret K. McElderberry Books, 2002)

Big Red Apple, Tony Johnston (Scholastic, 1999)

Caterpillar Fight, Sam McBratney (Candlewick Press/Scholastic, 1996)

Cookie's Week, Cindy Ward (Scholastic, 1988)

Dear Children of the Earth, Schim Schimmel (Northword Press Inc., 1994)

Differences, Gerard Arantowicz (Leathers Publishing, 2002)

Down on the Farm, Greg Scelsa (Creative Teaching Press, 1995)

Eating the Alphabet, Lois Ehlert (Scholastic, 1989)

Eyes, Nose, Fingers, and Toes, Judy Hindley (Candlewick Press, 1999)

Fall Leaves, Mary Packard (Scholastic, 1999)

FlannelGraphs, Jean Stangle (Fearon Teacher Aids. David S. Lake Publishers, 1986)

Flashing Fire Engine, Tony Mitten & Ant Parker (Scholastic, 1988)

Frog on a Log, Phil Roxbee Cox (Usborne Publishing, 2001)

From Head to Toe, Eric Carle (HarperCollins Publishers, 1997)

Going to the Dentist, Mercer Mayer (Golden Books Publishing Company, 1990)

GROUNDHOG DAY, Betsy Lewin (Aro Publishing Co., 1984)

Hand, Hand, Fingers, Thumb, Al Perkins (Random House, 1969)

Henrietta Circus Star, Sid Hoff (Garrard Publishing Company, 1978)

Hooray for St. Patrick's Day!, Joan Holub (Puffin Books, 2002)

How Do Dinosaurs Say Goodnight?, Jane Yolen. (Scholastic Inc. 2000)

Jamberry, Bruce Degen (Harper Trophy, 1983)

Just Like My Dad, Tricia Gardella (Caroline House Boyds Mills Press, 1993)

Merry Christmas, BIG HUNGRY BEAR!, Don & Audrey Wood (Blue Sky Press, 2002)

Mouse Paint, Ellen Stoll Walsh (Harcourt Brace & Co./Scholastic, 1989)

My Doctor, Harlow Rockwell (Macmillan Press, 1973)

One Little, Two Little, Three Little Pilgrims, B. G. Hennessy (Puffin Books, 1999)

Out of the Ocean, Debra Frasier (Scholastic, 1998)

Over in the Meadow, Olive A. Wadsworth & David Carter (Scholastic, 1992)

Pete's a Pizza, William Steig (HarperCollins Publishers/Scholastic, 1998)

Planting a Rainbow, Lois Ehlert (Voyager Books/Harcourt, 1988)

Pumpkin Heads, Wendell Minor (Scholastic, 2000)

Rain Song, Lezlie Evans (Scholastic, 1995)

Roaring Rocket, Tony Mitten & Ant Parker (Scholastic, 1997)

Stone Soup, Jon Muth (Scholastic Inc., 2003)

Stone Soup, Tony Ross (Fitzgerald, 2001)

Stranger in the Woods, Carl R. Sams II & Jean Stoick (Carl R. Sams II Photography, 2000)

Summer, Alice Low, illustrated by Roy McKie (Beginner Books, A Division of Random House, 1991)

The Great Easter Egg Hunt, Suzy-Jane Tanner (HarperCollins, 1996)

The Little Old Lady Who Was Not Afraid of Anything, Linda Williams (Scholastic, 1986)

The Mitten, Jan Brett (Scholastic, 1989)

The Shape of Things, Dayle Ann Dodds (Scholastic, 1994)

The Snow Tree, Caroline Repchuk (The Templar Company, 1996)

The Very Busy Spider, Eric Carle (Scholastic, 1984)

The Wind Blew, Pat Hutchins (Scholastic, 1974)

To Market, To Market, Anne Miranda (Harcourt Inc., 1997)

Turk and Runt, Lisa Wheeler (Antheneum Books for Young Readers, 2002)

Twelve Days of Christmas, Jan Brett (Trumpet Club, 1992)

Valentines, Judith Moffatt (Scholastic, 1999)

White Rabbit's Color Book, Alan Baker (Houghton Mifflin Company, 1999)

Window Music, Anastasia Suen (Puffin Books, 1998)

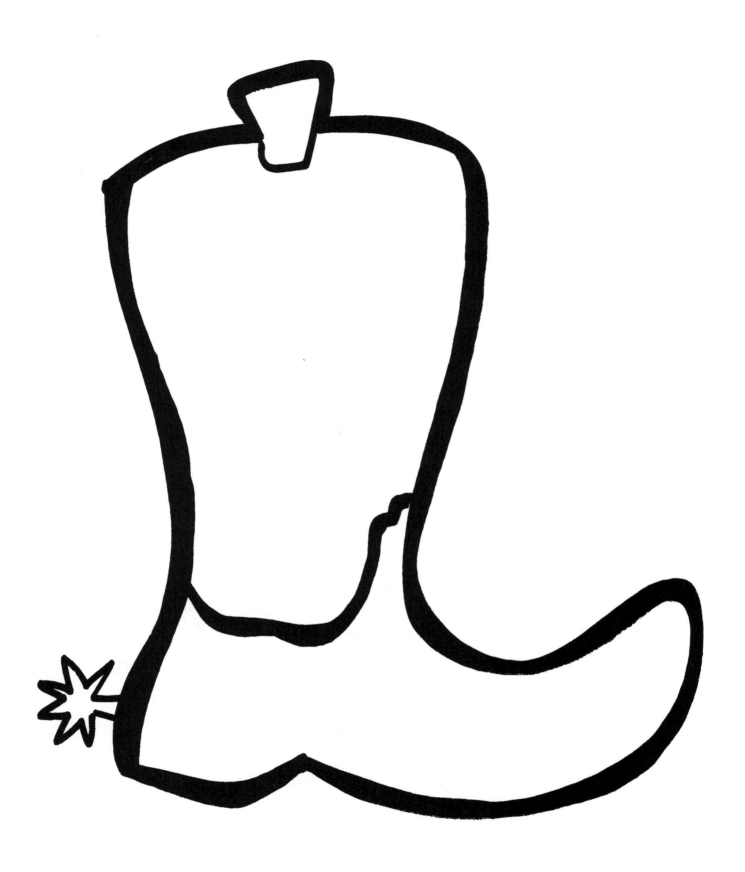

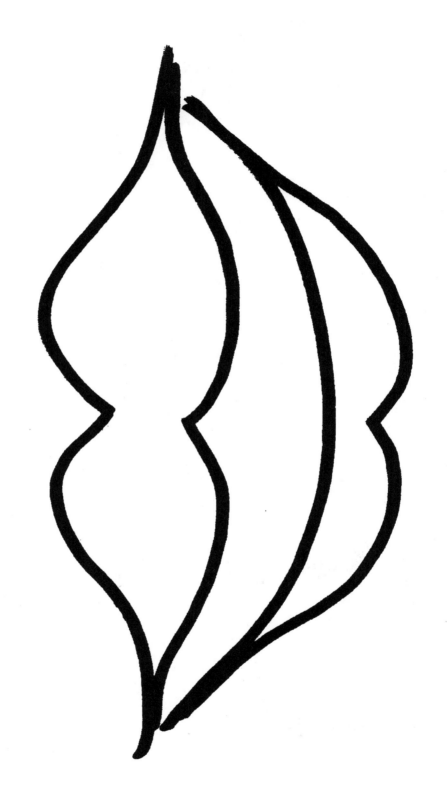

162 Learn to Move, Move to Learn!

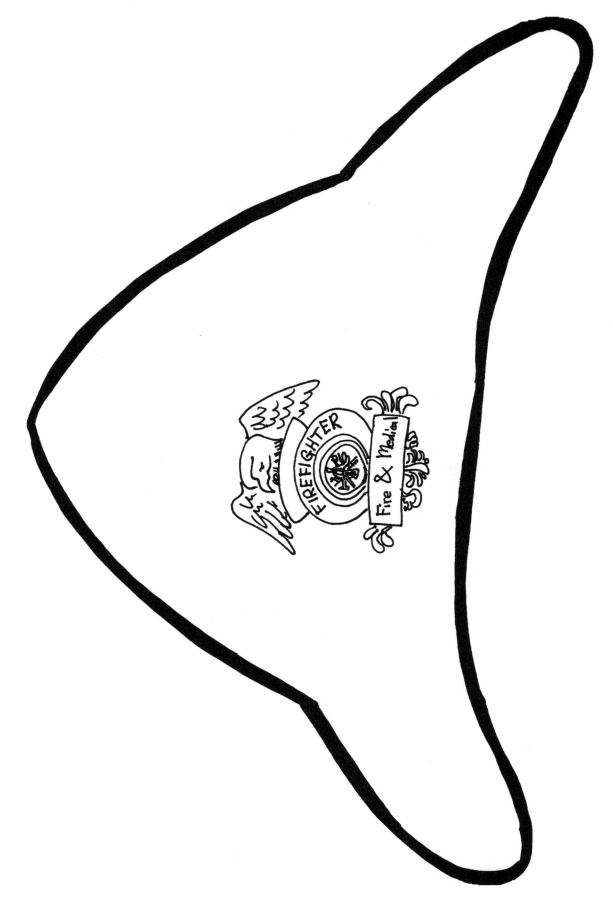

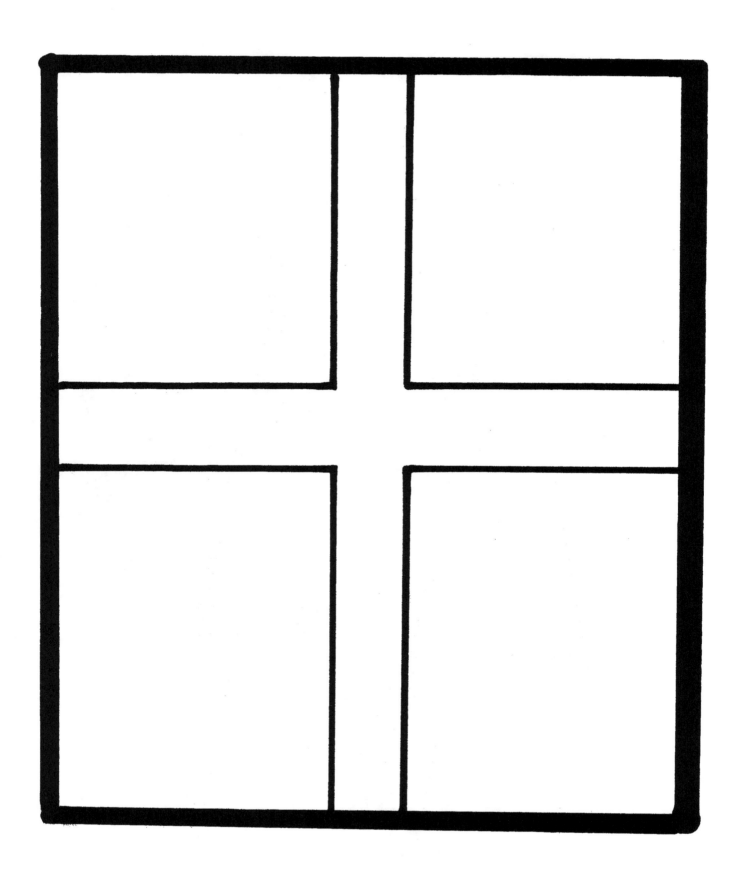

170 Learn to Move, Move to Learn!

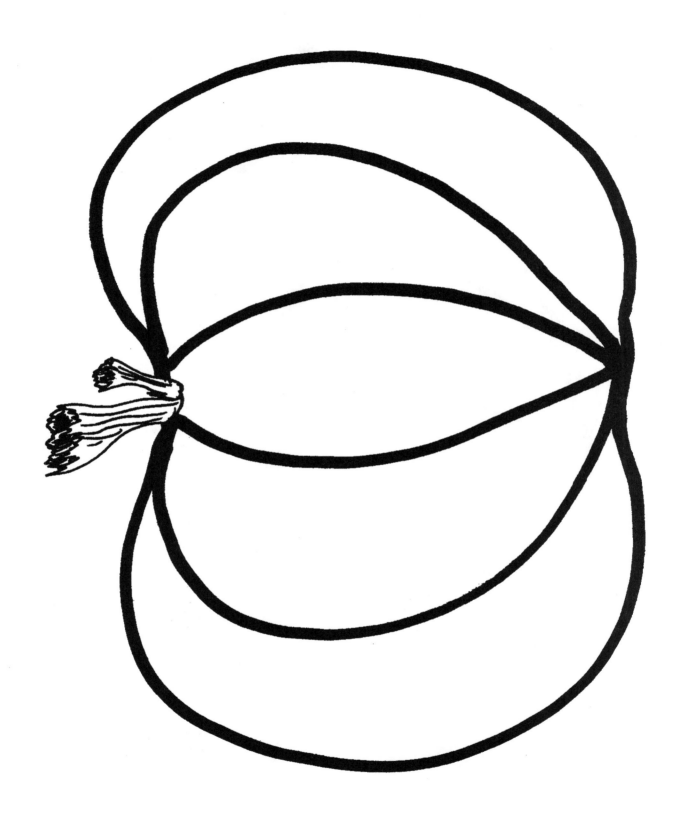

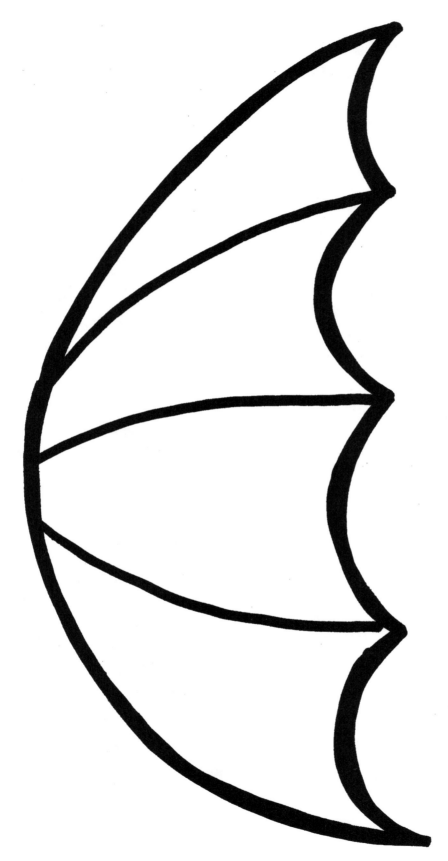

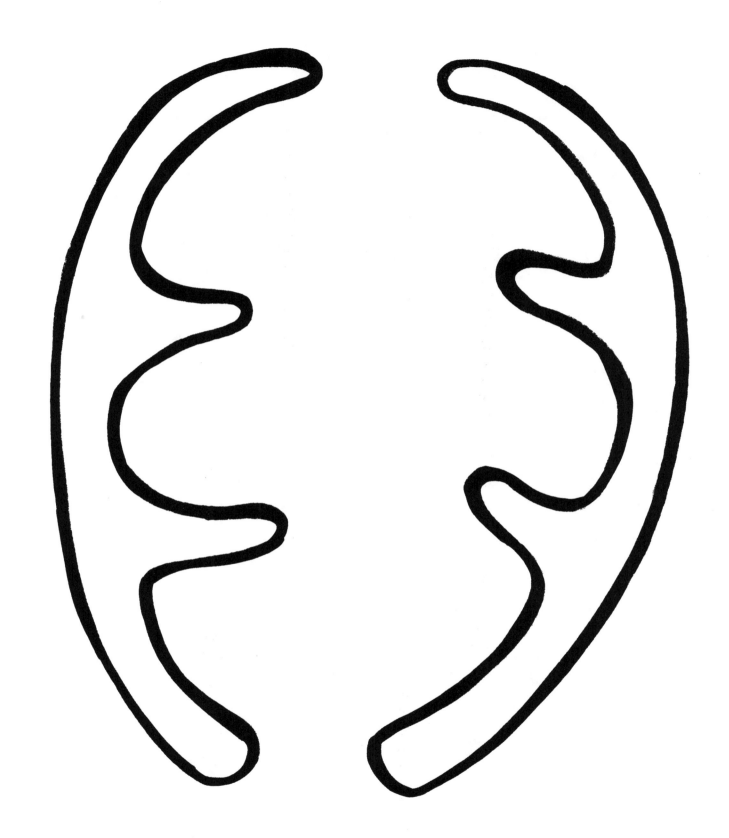

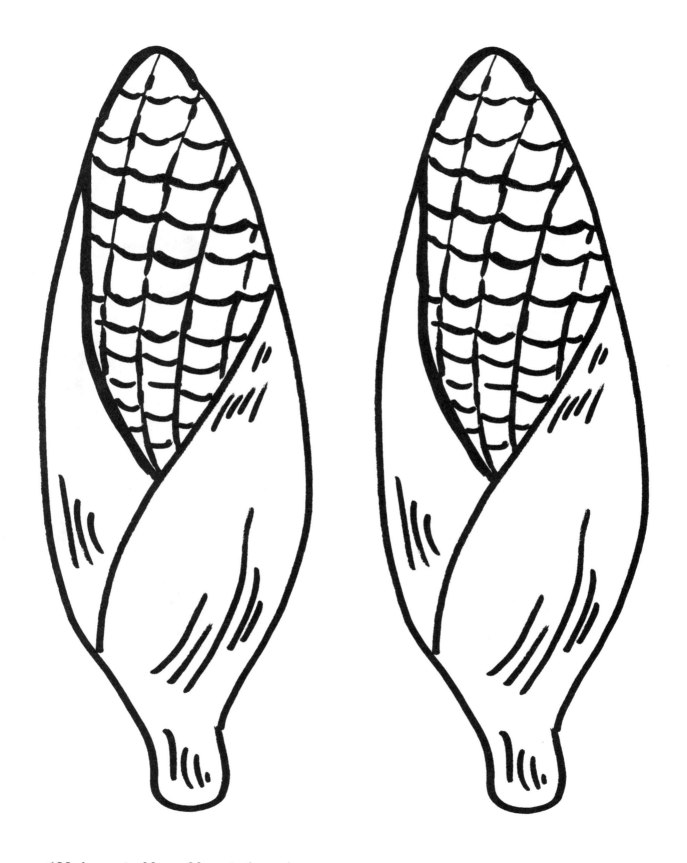

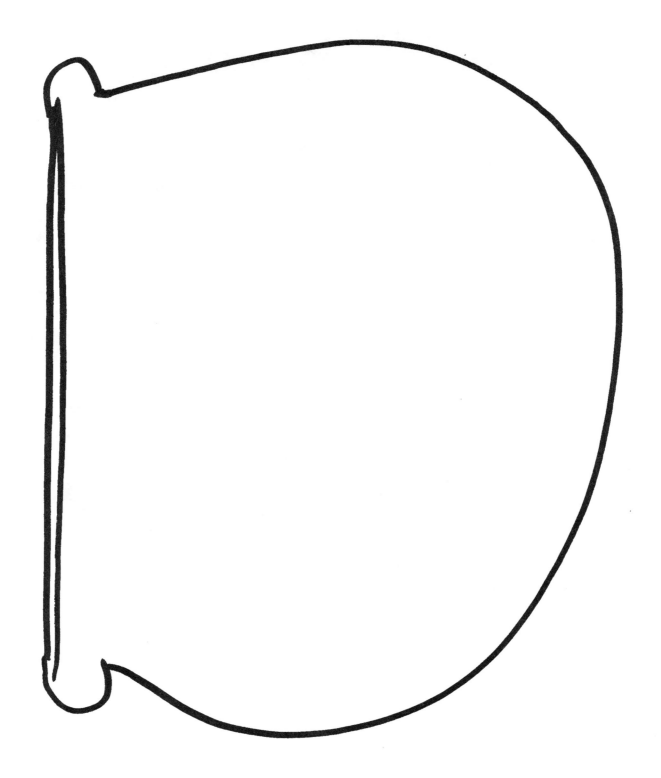

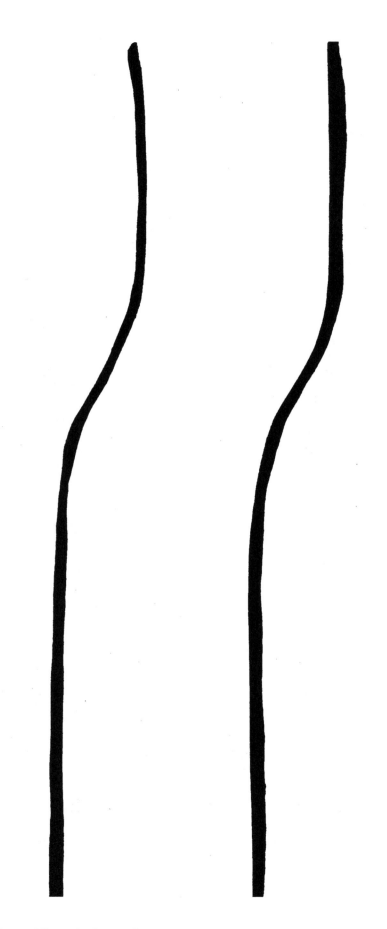

186 Learn to Move, Move to Learn!